TRANSFORMATIVE TRAVEL IN NEPAL

FULFILLING A DREAM IN THE HIMALAYAS

By

Kate Benzin

First printing, July 2012

Printed in the United States of America

What Others Have Said About

Transformative Travel in Nepal

"**Really Great Book!!** I thoroughly enjoyed reading this book about Kate's journey with her friend Kay to the Himalayas. First I loved reading Kate's history. She's an independent person who has had many adventures in life and seems fearless. This book describes how she realized her dream of trekking in the Himalayas. It's also a book about personal growth, uncertainty, courage and victory. It's also about FUN!" – Sandy Bose

"**Very Engaging Book**, I thoroughly enjoyed reading about the author's adventure in the Himalayas. This book is very well-written, and the author's account of the trip of her dreams is fascinating. I felt as if I were right there with her the entire time." – Avid Reader

"**What an Adventurer!** Fantastic and interesting account of one woman's journey to the Himalayas. This story is well writtten and will encourage every well-intentioned traveler to get up off the couch and follow his or her dream on the map of life. A gutsy trip that proves you can accomplish any goal you set out for yourself." - Magic

Other Books

By

Kate Benzin

Kindle and Paperback:

How To Find The Heart Of Bali

The Modern Nomad
(available August 2012)

October 2012 – Look for the next book in the Modern Nomad series which discusses how to work and still be a nomad.

Dedication

Fulfilling my lifelong dream of trekking in the Himalayas was a turning point in my life, and I would like to thank three people for helping me fulfill this dream.

First is Kay – my good friend, my diving buddy, my trekking partner, my traveling-everywhere partner. She has always been most patient with me through all our travels – even when she had every right to clobber me over the head to try to knock some sense into me. Thanks for your patience.

Second is Furwa, our guide on the Langtang trek. He provided much needed common sense guidance that made it possible for us to get through each day without giving up and to appreciate our hardships for the lessons they presented to us. Thanks for your guidance.

And third is Gurung, our Sherpa who carried all our supplies – even the cosmetics that I needed in order to feel I could present myself to the world each day. It was incredible to watch him every day scampering around those rugged mountains in his flip-flops with both of our backpacks on his slight frame! Thanks for your help.

Table of Contents

Foreword

I have traveled with Kate many times and we've had many exciting experiences. But the adventure that she describes in this book was definitely one of the most thrilling, awe inspiring, and fulfilling that either one of us had ever experienced.

To this day, looking back on the Langtang trek that we did fills me with wonder at what we accomplished.

We left the U.S. very spontaneously, not really knowing what to expect. I had done my share of hiking in the Appalachian and the Rocky Mountains in the U.S. and figured it would probably be a little more difficult. What I had not taken into consideration was that we were going into the highest and the most beautiful mountains in the world.

The experiences that we had in those mountains left an indelible impression on me, and I will always be thankful that I answered the phone the day that Kate called and our trip was born.

Kay Johnson

Colorado Springs, CO

Kate Benzin

Introduction

I think I'm goin' to Kathmandu
I think it's really where I'm goin' to
Hey, if I ever get out of here
That what I'm gonna do

K-k-k-k-k-k-Kathmandu
I think it's really where I'm goin' to
Hey, if I ever get out of here
I'm goin' to Kathmandu

Song by Bob Seger

How many people have ended up going to Kathmandu because they just couldn't get that Bob Seger song out of their minds? I thought that it must be a really wonderful place to have such a great song celebrating it. And man, that singer really wanted to go. I wonder if he ever got there.

I had a dream of going to Kathmandu and trekking in the Himalayas long before I heard that song. I really do not know how serious I was about ever getting there, but once I heard that song, I could not get Kathmandu out of my mind. Over and over it played. You know how that is when you wake up in the middle of the night and a particular song is going through your brain again and again. Then you're sitting at breakfast. Yep, you guessed it – same song re-playing itself for the umpteenth and umpteenth and one times.

So I had to go – I didn't have a choice. Maybe if I went to Kathmandu, then I would be able to get that song out of my brain and finally bring some peace and quiet back to my head again.

But my long-standing dream of heading to Kathmandu to do some trekking in the Himalayas was one that seemed impossible. After all, it was a location so exotic that I could not even conjure up what it would feel like to be there – to set my feet on land that was unexplored by any Westerners except the most curious and gutsy.

Kathmandu was and is backpacker mecca and the staging point for anyone planning to go trekking in the Himalayas. You may have had some friends who had the same dream as me. Maybe it has been one of your dreams as well?? Or do you have a different dream – one that you have lived with for a long time but never seriously thought you could fulfill?

Signs in Thamel, Kathmandu
from igougo.com

If you picked up this book, then maybe somewhere deep inside of you, there is a bell ringing that is telling you "Now is the time to do something about achieving your dream – whatever that dream might be."

-Have you ever dreamed about walking on land that very few other Westerners have or will ever set foot on?

-Have you ever wondered how great it would be to see the Himalayan mountains up close – picture-perfect locations that can only be experienced in person after trekking for days and days?

-Would you like to push yourself to do more physically as well as mentally than you ever thought possible?

-Do you have your own secret dream that is on your bucket list to do?

Maybe you are just about ready to do something more than dream about it. Maybe you are ready to step outside your comfort zone, break away from the role that you have been taught, and take charge of finding exactly what will fulfill you.

If you are ready to discover that truth – if you are ready to face the possibility of achieving something that you never thought possible, then read on. Maybe the story of how I dared to satisfy my hunger to wake up in the morning with the majestic Himalayas outside my window so close that it seemed possible to reach my hand out and touch them will inspire you to fulfill your own dream as well.

It is a bit hazy when my dream of trekking in the Himalayas started. I remember reading the classic adventure book <u>Lost Horizons</u> when I was very young, perhaps around 14 years old. I was entranced by the romance of it all and the idea of some far off land where life was perfect. Like many teenagers, I felt that life had been a big disappointment. What was the purpose anyway?

Why did I have to study boring subjects? Why couldn't I just study subjects that actually interested me? Life would be so wonderful if I did not have to follow so many rules imposed by others.

Yes, the Shangri-la of <u>Lost Horizons</u> where peace and happiness were the norm was the place I wanted to be. What a paradise! In my young girl's imagination, I still thought that anything was possible. So yes, I thought that it was feasible to live somewhere without all the emotional ups and downs of everyday living that I was experiencing as a teenager in the U.S.

The setting seemed to be in the Himalayas, so I think that is when I started dreaming about going there. It is not important that I know when or how the dream started. What is important is simply having a fantasy of some sort and then recognizing the perfect time to fulfill it – or at least to do my best to fulfill it.

It was not my only dream, but it was definitely the longest running one. If I had been put on the spot about whether I would ever actually do any trekking in the Himalayas and see those gorgeous mountains up close and personal, I am sure I would have said no, that it was just a fantasy.

Like many people, I kept this dream pretty much to myself and did nothing consciously to make it come true. Instead, I just kept it in a secret place where it was mine alone to comfort me when I was feeling depressed or when I just wanted to daydream about escaping.

I guess it was kind of like the dream lots of people have of winning the lottery. We all love to fantasize about what we will do with all the money we get when we win that big prize even though most of us are realistic enough to understand that it is pretty certain that we have virtually no chance at that. But what a luscious escape it is to dream about it.

And what I did not know at the time that I went trekking in the Himalayas was how that trip would transform my attitude about what I could achieve – it was truly 'transformative travel.' It is not that I lacked confidence in myself prior to this adventure. In fact, even as I look back on who I was then, I see a woman who was secure enough to risk her security in her search for happiness and fulfillment, a woman who followed many avenues that others might have thought dangerous or reckless.

The day after graduation from college, instead of sticking around home, I got into a car to drive out to Los Angeles for a teaching job.

A few years later, I gave up tenure as a teacher in Los Angeles without anything else certain waiting in the wings.

Some years after that, I took a leave of absence from graduate school to go off for a 3-month work assignment in Indonesia – a country that I knew virtually nothing about at the time.

No, I had enough confidence in myself to feel that I could handle pretty much whatever was thrown my way. That does not mean that I really could handle all that, but at least I thought that I could.

When fate stepped into my life and presented the opportunity to go to Kathmandu, it was unexpected. My friend Kay and I had jokingly talked about getting fit over the winter. That idea of getting in shape was not the goal, but we basically just used it as an excuse for an opportunity to travel to an exotic destination.

It gave us the cover story. I told friends that we were going off on a fabulous adventure – and oh yeah, it was not just a frivolous decision because we were going to be working hard at getting into great physical shape!

Like many Americans, I had spent most of my life in sedentary mode. And like many people, I kept telling myself that I should exercise more. I bought memberships at gyms, but only used them once or twice and then let the membership cards sit on my desk at home.

I had more fitness books than the public library. I also had more fitness videos than any of the local gyms where I had my non-memberships. A friend of mine once said that I got more exercise just moving the exercise videos from one shelf to another than I ever did in using them.

My friend was right. I got out of breath walking up just one flight of stairs. And even though I could barely hold a conversation and walk at the same time at sea level, I did nothing to get fit.

So there I was – overweight, out of shape, 54 years old – with this wonderful dream that I thought would probably never be fulfilled. But then a series of unrelated events unfolded that led me in a roundabout way to fulfill my dream of trekking in the Himalayas.

So now let me share with you how it all came about. And I hope by doing so, I can help you realize your own dreams.

Kate Benzin

PART 1
GETTING
READY

Kate Benzin

Chapter 1- Before

Twenty years from now you will be more disappointed by the things you didn't do than by the ones you did do. So throw off the bowlines, sail away from the safe harbor. Catch the trade winds in your sails. Explore. Dream. Discover. – Mark Twain

Even though I did not realize it at the time, I was following Mark Twain's advice in 1982 when I moved to Indonesia on a lark for a three-month job contract. It certainly was not the safe thing to do, but making that move fulfilled my needs of the moment.

You see at that time, I was in my late 30's and had gone back to graduate school to become a clinical psychologist. But I felt as though a noose was tightening around my neck – once I set up practice as a psychologist, I would have to stay put in one place. I would never be able to find out what it was like to explore the world, something I had always wanted to do.

So when a short assignment in exotic Indonesia appeared, I said to myself "What the hell – it's only three months" and took a leave of absence from grad school and headed to Indonesia to sew some wild oats – a little later in life than most, but I was divorced and had no children, so why not do as Mark Twain said to "throw off the bowlines, sail away from the safe harbor."

That short assignment started in December 1982. As I write this in June 2012, I am still in Indonesia, which has become my home for most of the past 30 years. Obviously, following Mark Twain's advice worked for me, and it might work for you as well.

Meeting Kay – Future Traveling Partner

Meeting Kay in 1994 was one step toward fulfilling my dream even though I did not recognize it at the time. I was living in Indonesia, teaching English as a foreign language at ILP (International Language Program), a large private language school in Jakarta, the bustling capital of Indonesia.

One day at school, I was idly talking to a fellow teacher about scuba diving. I did not realize it, but another teacher that I did not yet know overheard me as she walked past my desk. She came back later to talk to me about diving. She was also a diver and suggested that we do some diving together. That person was Kay, and that was the start of a beautiful friendship.

Indonesia and other parts of Southeast Asia have some world-class diving sites. So Kay and I bonded as we explored dive sites in the area. We subsequently became lifelong friends and travel partners, as well as dive buddies, traveling to many parts of Indonesia and other parts of Southeast Asia for diving and just general exploring.

We soon found that we were both the same kind of traveler. We were not into five-star accommodations and fine dining, even if we could have afforded it. On the contrary, we were backpacker types and were willing to stay in whatever no-star accommodations we could find.

Even after Kay left Indonesia, we kept in touch and traveled together whenever we could. We usually managed to take a trip to an exotic destination every four to five years or so.

Any Job for Six Months a Year

By this time, I was in my early 50's, but still hadn't found my perfect work niche. I'd had many career changes since graduating college in 1966, but nothing suited me or attracted me to stick to it permanently.

Spanish teacher in Los Angeles

All kinds of secretarial and administrative office work at many different kinds of firms and in many different cities

Kate Benzin

Technical editor

Customer service representative

English teacher in Indonesia

Waitress

Graduate student in psychology

Limousine driver

And many more

The only item on that list that I really loved was being a graduate student in psychology. But I knew that being a clinical psychologist would not give me enough time off every year to do some serious traveling. I knew that once I set up practice as a clinical psychologist, I would find it difficult to tell clients, "Oh, yeah. By the way, I'm leaving for a 6-month holiday."

You see, I had another dream besides going to the Himalayas. I wanted to have several months of freedom every year. I wanted the luxury of choice during my months off. Maybe I would travel. Maybe I would learn how to play piano. Maybe I would spend the time oil painting. The important thing was that the choice would be mine. What delicious freedom that would be!

No, I have always hated the idea of putting up with two-week vacations once a year. My travels had to be a minimum of three months long – and preferably longer. In fact, I told anyone who would listen that I would do anything for six months a year if it gave me the rest of the year free. In other words, if cleaning toilets paid enough during six months to support me for the entire year, then I would do that.

You can see that unlike a lot of people, I was not looking for fulfillment in my work. I did not think that there was a job that would provide the kind of all round satisfaction that I craved. I knew that I needed freedom to look for gratification and a fully satisfying and exhilarating life wherever the search led me.

Of course, it is obvious that it is very difficult to find a job that allows an employee to take six months off every year. So I muddled along from job to job – not finding what I was looking for.

Teaching English in Indonesia

It was really just by chance that I ended up teaching English as a foreign language in Indonesia. When my short-term job training Indonesians on word processing equipment ended, I took the only kind of job that I felt that I could reasonably do – teaching a foreign language – only in this case the foreign language was English.

I had been a Spanish teacher in Los Angeles right after graduation from college, but had hated it. I am sure that a large part of the problem was that I was still young and immature and wanted to have fun. I was not ready to get serious about making a living or facing the transition from being a student to being a teacher. After all, it was the late 1960's, and I had just left Illinois for a job in Los Angeles – the promised land to many of us in those days.

Also – and this is key to being a happy teacher – my students were not really motivated. They were taking Spanish because most colleges in those days required students to have two years of a foreign language in order to be accepted. And since Spanish was considered the easiest foreign language, many high school students who considered they might have college in their futures took Spanish instead of something more difficult. This situation did not make for a stimulating environment for me as a teacher.

But I did love the camaraderie I felt among the teachers and have often missed that feeling over the years.

Still, after my experience teaching Spanish in the L.A. school system, I had sworn that I would never teach again. However, when my original job in Indonesia ended and I wanted to stay in the country, teaching English was the easiest job to find. I figured that if I could teach Spanish, then I certainly should be able to teach my own language using the same methods I had learned for teaching Spanish.

And teaching English turned out very well for me. First of all, I was older and more mature – ready to accept my role as teacher. In addition, most of my students were adults who were really motivated to learn English because they knew that being proficient in English would help them out in their career paths.

Another advantage was that I signed contracts for a year at a time. This appealed to my wanderlust and need for freedom – I was not "tied down," so I could always move on again at the end of a year-long contract if I wanted to. It seemed the perfect balance – enough of a commitment to be interesting, but not so much that I felt trapped.

Becoming a Student Again

And then one day, fate took over – I was in the right place at the right time.

It was July 1995. And there I was – sitting in the reception area of the language school where I was teaching English at the time, and a young woman by the name of Ann came in. I assumed that she was a teacher looking for work, but she said, "No, I'm a tour director."

Some friends of mine had actually suggested this line of work to me in the past, but I had told them they were crazy – that they didn't know me very well if they thought I was going to babysit a bunch of old people on some bus tour. The word 'tour' was definitely a four-letter word to me for a long time as it was the opposite of solo travel and adventurous exploring.

But when Ann said those words to me, it was as if an apple fell on my head – lights went off – I had an epiphany. And I said to myself, "That's exactly what I'm going to do."

Shortly after meeting Ann, I had the chance to do some research about tour directing while I was on a short trip to the US. Wow! All I had to do was take a two-week intensive course in Denver – and presto change-o – I would become a tour director.

I did not even realize yet that tour directing would give me my cherished six months off every year – or maybe even longer. But even without that incentive, I was now drawn to the idea of going into this career and so immediately signed up for the course.

Being a Tour Director

While I was getting established as a tour director, I stayed in the U.S. for a few years. I felt that a reputable tour operator would look more favorably on a resume that had a U.S. address as opposed to an address in Indonesia. Tour operators fly the tour director to the starting point of each tour, and most tour directors start out working stateside. It would not have been a good business decision for a tour operator to fly me from Indonesia to the U.S. for tours.

It is only after a tour director has become fairly experienced that he or she is given international assignments. And once the tour director is working internationally, he or she can usually live anywhere in the world as long as the tour operator conducts international tours.

While living in the U.S., I worked for a couple of tour operators and found that yes, indeed, I had quite a bit of time off every year – in fact, more than six months. You might think that would make me happy. But unfortunately, I was not getting enough tours to make enough money to support me during the time that I was not working. I was afraid that this was just not going to work out.

In addition to not having enough work, I was not making much money on the tours either. You see, a tour director's income comes mostly from gratuities extended by the tour guests at the end of the tour. So a tour director needs to work for a high end tour operator with generous clients in order to survive financially during the off-season.

So while I was working for these first two tour operators, I had to work in the off-season as well. The possibility of having half a year off went down the drain.

I started to think that my decision to become a tour director had been a bad one. I was not sorry that I had given it a try, but having to take jobs in the off-season in order to survive meant that I was not any closer to having my precious six months off every year. And leading tours is far more stressful than teaching English in Indonesia. So I was debating what I should do.

I recognized that working for the current two tour operators was not working out. Was there a tour operator that could give me enough work with upscale guests to make it financially viable? I was not sure.

The teacher at my tour director training course had repeatedly recommended a particular tour operator, which for the sake of avoiding any law suits, I will call *Bradley Tours*. But the problem was that Bradley required their tour directors to work six months without any days off. Initially, I did not think I could do that. So even though Bradley had expressed interest in me when I sent them my resume, I had ignored their request for more information.

But since I couldn't make enough money working on and off during the six-month-long tour season, then it seemed that the only way to make enough money was if I worked non-stop during those popular tour months May through October. Then perhaps I would have enough money to survive the other half year. Obviously, there were other tour directors who were doing it – if they could do it, maybe I could as well.

Could I? I decided to give it a try. And if it did not work out, then I would head back to Indonesia and teach English again. At least I had that to fall back on.

Light at the End of the Tunnel

I finished my first season with Bradley, and I could see the light at the end of the tunnel. This company gave me enough work, the tour guests were generous, and the result was that I was able to make enough money to have my first precious six months off. When my tour season ended in November 1998, I knew that I was free until the following spring, and I was in heaven.

Now I just had to figure out what I was going to do with my free time? Since I had not been able to survive in the off-season during my first two years as a tour director, I was taken by surprise with my new status – I could manage financially over the winter without working. How thrilling!!

But I was not ready with a plan. It is amazing how we ache for something and then do not know how to deal with it once we get it! But I was going to take advantage of this freedom – one way or another.

Somewhere in my sub-conscious, I still had my dream of going to the Himalayas. I was 54 years old, significantly overweight, and totally out of shape. I still could not walk and talk at the same time at sea level without getting out of breath! And just how high were those Himalayas anyhow??

If I had consciously thought about going to the Himalayas at that point, I would have put it back into the secret box once again. I was not really in a position to fulfill this dream of trekking in the Himalayas. It was too unrealistic. Why didn't I do it when I was much younger and still thin? I was not in shape then either, but it would have been much easier to deal with the stress of extreme physical activity while I was still a size 9!

I had been dreaming about the Himalayas for a very long time. When I moved to Indonesia in 1982, friends laughed at me for taking along my down jacket and hiking boots to a tropical destination. But when I first went there for that three-month assignment, I unrealistically had figured that, being in Asia, I would be so much closer to Nepal that surely I would be able to manage a side trip to do some trekking.

Of course, my grasp of geography at that time left much to be desired. Indonesia was much further from Nepal and the Himalayas than I had imagined. And that little side trip for trekking did not happen.

The Phone Call

So there I was at the end of my tour season looking at six free months, but floundering around, not knowing what to do with my free time. Well, at least I could phone my friend and traveling buddy Kay to catch up with her. Fate again!

I called Kay just to chat. I had no intention of suggesting a trip of any sort. I did not even know whether she was free to travel. I told her that I was at loose ends and not sure what I was going to do over the winter before I would start leading tours again the following spring. I did not have any proposals or suggestions. We were just chatting.

Then she casually mentioned that her plan was to get fit over the winter. I just as casually jokingly replied, "We could get fit trekking in the Himalayas." And a trip was born. It was just as quick as that. Before I could say "We could get fit trekking in the Himalayas" three times and click our heels, we were heading to Nepal.

Fortune had smiled on us – we were both in a position to take off right away. All we had to do was to get flights and be on our way. So within three weeks, we were on a plane to begin our new adventure.

In the little guidebook reading that we did before getting on the plane, we found out that this was definitely not the right time of year for trekking in the Himalayas. We were going at the coldest time of the year and would be staying overnight in 'teahouses' that had no hot water and no heating. But for some reason, that did not even put a dent in our non-strategy. You go when you are ready to go regardless of the circumstances.

How does a woman like me usually prepare for trekking in the Himalayas, the highest mountains in the world? Well, she would normally make plans several months in advance so that she would have time to go down to her local gym and enroll in one of every strenuous class offered, especially if, to date, her most physically demanding effort generally involved lifting her fork to her mouth.

However, since our departure was so spontaneous, neither Kay nor I had a moment to spare for such a minor technicality as getting into appropriate physical condition. Of course, Kay was not nearly as overweight as me. She was in much better physical shape than I was, and she lived at 6,000 feet altitude in Colorado. So she had several advantages over me, but I was fulfilling a lifelong dream – what I lacked in the way of preparation I more than made up for with enthusiasm.

Fate Again

A friend of mine named Lynn had lived and worked in Nepal after getting divorced. What a stroke of luck for me – not her divorce, but her experiences in Nepal!

She was a real fitness buff and had gone to Nepal trekking - ended up loving it so much that she moved there and started teaching English as a foreign language in Kathmandu.

She was no longer in Nepal, but I decided to ask her advice about what I would need to do to get into good enough shape for trekking in the Himalayas. Amazingly, she told me to do nothing - just get out trekking and get in shape on the trek. She said that the first few days would be very difficult, but that it would get easier each day.

OK - that was easy for her to say since she was already in very good condition when she went on her very first trek. But what about me?

She knew me very well, but even though I knew that she recognized my shortcomings, I felt that she was not really being realistic about what I could accomplish. But since her advice was actually just what I really wanted to hear anyway, I decided to take her completely at her word and go for it. Why should I be a non-believer in her strategy? I guess somewhere deep inside of me I felt that I could blame her if it did not work out well.

Fortunately, I did not let it register in my brain that not only was I going to be subjected to greater physical demands than I had ever experienced before, but that I would be trekking in the off season, at the coldest time of year, to areas that would have no electricity and no heat.

How would I deal with the altitude, the cold, the exertion? The only way to find the answer to that question was to plunge in at the deep end and "just do it" in the words of Nike.

So Kay and I headed for the Himalayas.

Kate Benzin

‿

Chapter 2 - Getting Started

*For me, travel represents freedom. I have freedom of location, sure, but also the freedom to communicate with whomever I want, and to not communicate with those I don't want to keep in touch with. I have the freedom to wake up and go to sleep when I want, and to decide how long to stay in a given place and when I should leave, breaking my established habits and routines. - Colin Wright, author, **How to Travel Full Time***

Kathmandu

Some people choose to trek in the Himalayas with a tour operator that conducts all-inclusive packages, but trekkers, who are often very adventurous types, often prefer to do things spontaneously instead of following well-designed plans.

Kay and I fall into that second group, and so it was not surprising that we arrived in Kathmandu without any plans. I did not care. We had dropped down into a world so different and exotic that I was happy to have time just to wander around the city before even starting to think seriously about trekking.

Cows and goats were roaming the streets. Taxis were cheap piles of junk hobbling along, stinking and wheezing. Cars, trucks, motorcycles, bicycles, pushcarts, rickshaws, ox carts, stray dogs were all fighting for space on the narrow roads, weaving their way in and out. Drivers beeped their horns so often that it was impossible to know when the beeping was meant for you.

The thing that really got to me as a dog lover were all the sad-looking dogs that were the least cared for that I had ever seen anywhere in the world. And the eyes of Buddha were everywhere, giving the place an other-worldly feel. See the next photo for a glimpse of the eyes of Buddha. They are on temples all over Kathmandu.

Kathmandu, with a population close to 1 million, is the capital of Nepal. More importantly for trekkers, it is the central meeting point for everyone planning to go trekking anywhere in the Himalayas. In fact, many people do the same thing that Kay and I did – just show up in Kathmandu with no fixed plans. This is because it is very easy to arrange everything necessary for a trek within just a few days in Thamel, the backpacker and tourism center of Kathmandu.

Guides can be found at most of the local watering holes. In addition, they put up their contact information at bulletin boards all over Thamel. Now it is possible to arrange all of this online, but in 1998, the internet had not yet taken the world by storm. Besides, I would still want to interview the guide in person unless he came with a really good recommendation from a close friend. There are probably 100 or more guides available for every trekker. How do you choose which one is best for you? If you do not have a recommendation from a friend, then you just have to use your instincts.

It is not even necessary for trekkers to bring their own supplies because every trekking necessity is available at local outfitter stores at prices far more reasonable than in the West.

The ideal time for trekking is either April-May or September-October because those months have weather that is not too cold and not too hot, but we arrived in December. That was when we had time available, and we were not worried about Mother Nature anyway. I tend to be the kind of person who expects everything to just work out one way or another. I guess that means that I am a glass-half-full rather than half-empty kind of girl. In any case, I have found that flying by the seat of my pants is the style that suits me just fine.

Even though Thamel was not overrun with travelers because it was the off-season, we met trekkers who had just come off the trail and some who were getting ready to hit the trail. Kay and I chatted with anyone who was willing to talk about their experiences on trek and with anyone who was willing to share advice they had been given.

I am sure that everyone could tell that we were total novices, but I did not care. I felt privileged that we were talking to trekkers who had been to Everest base camp. I did not have a prayer of doing that, but I was still interested in hearing about the difficulties and the thrills of such a difficult endeavor.

So Kay and I spent the first several days walking around Thamel, breathing the polluted air, getting advice, and looking for the best deals on the essential down accessories – sleeping bags, jackets, booties, etc.

I had brought my own sleeping bag, down jacket, and hiking boots, but since I am a real shopaholic, a large part of the fun for me was going around to all the outfitting stores to see what was available and replace much of what I had brought from the U.S. with improved versions of the same things. After all, shouldn't I have the best equipment possible? I'm worth it!

I bought a better sleeping bag, a decision that I would later applaud over and over again during the cold nights on the trail. I added a down vest that I could wear under my Goretex jacket when necessary, but ended up using it mostly for sleeping. I also added a few items to my growing stockpile, most notably a pair of down booties which also earned my undying gratitude.

Given that I am a such a shopper and always prefer having more rather than less, it is pretty amazing to me that I did not even consider the possibility that I might need a walking stick. Yes, I saw them everywhere, and a couple of shop owners even tried to sell them to me. But I thought those sticks were only necessary for the really difficult treks. And we certainly were not going to choose one of those. We would pick a baby trek to start with. But even though we chose a relatively easy trek, we would find out just how important walking sticks were. Luckily by that time, we had been given the local bamboo version sticks.

Making Some Serious Decisions

Eventually, we were ready to get serious about choosing our first trek and getting out of Kathmandu to get on the trail. There are so many established treks to choose from that it can be a bit overwhelming to decide which one would be easy enough for a beginner like me and yet not be so easy that people in the know would laugh behind my back. Of course, I did not realize it at the time, but there are no treks that fall into that category. They are all difficult for a novice like me.

We also had a couple of guidebooks that we casually browsed through. Lots of treks sounded wonderful, and they all sounded difficult, but we decided on the *Langtang* trek.

During the prime trekking season of April-May and September-October, the trails can actually get fairly crowded, especially on the popular treks in Annapurna and Everest regions. Accommodations at teahouses can even sometimes be full. Since we were trekking in late December and since the Langtang trek was not as popular as the treks in those two regions, we were pretty sure that we would have our choice of accommodations at the teahouses along the way. In fact, we wondered just how many intrepid souls like us we would encounter on the trail.

The Langtang trek was fairly close to Kathmandu. The starting point was only a 10-hour bus ride away over rough roads – we would find out later just how very rough they were.

Maybe its proximity to Kathmandu was part of its initial allure. But there was more. Some trekkers that we met in a Thamel restaurant had told us how beautiful it was with gorgeous views of the snow-capped peaks of the Himalayas. They also said that it was an easy trek! I would have liked to have been able to say a few choice words to them once Kay and I finished that very trek. They must have been mountain goats in another life!

Regardless, now that the decision about which trek to do had been made, we needed someone to carry our packs. We both figured that we could handle our own daypacks, but not the heavy backpacks that held our sleeping bags, extra clothing, towels, and of course my cosmetics. There was no way I was going to face each day without putting on my face!

Kay and I consulted with Angela, a friend living in Kathmandu that I had met a few years before. We wanted her advice about finding a porter. Kay had indicated a willingness to carry her own backpack in addition to her daypack. I thought she was crazy, and I certainly was not going down that road. I was definitely not carrying my backpack on my first trek.

So I knew we needed a porter. But we were not in the market for a guide as well. After all, couldn't we find our own way. Didn't we just have to follow the instructions in the guidebook? According to what we had read, there were enough trekkers on the trail to make it pretty obvious where the trail actually was – even in the off-season. And the guidebooks made it clear that the locals were used to having trekkers in their world, knew the paths, and were more than happy to point out the right way to any confused trekker.

But evidently, this was just the way it was done – guide and porter combo. That was the deal – take it or leave it. And the price for the duo was so low that it did not take much convincing for us to agree to hire both. The deal was done and we would soon be on our way. And I would be particularly happy that we had hired both – once the guide took my daypack to help me out at a particularly difficult spot, I never carried it again! That was heaven!

So we hired Furwa as guide and Sherpa Gurung as porter, a team that often worked together. Neither one of them looked brawny enough to carry even one of our backpacks, but we soon found out that Gurung would be carrying both of our backpacks – at the same time. And he would do that while blithely scampering over the uneven ground in his flip flops.

Furwa, on the other hand, had a proper pair of hiking boots, a gift from a previous client as I later learned. The difference in footwear was also a reflection of the difference in their status – a guide has higher status than a porter. Even though I saw no major difference in how they were treated at the teahouses, there were nuances that a trained eye would notice, like the difference in footwear or the deference that Gurung always paid Furwa.

Lesson learned: there is a reason the locals do what they do. Before you swim against the tide, make sure you know why all the salmon are swimming the other way – especially in a foreign land and different culture. Don't insist on doing what you are used to doing in the U.S. After all, that is the reason you are traveling – to expand your horizons, to learn to be more flexible, and to sink yourself in a different culture.

Gurung & Furwa
Scanned from a 13-year-old photo

Chapter 3 - The Himalayas: Where Earth Meets Sky

In these hills, Nature's hospitality eclipses all men can ever do. The enchanting beauties of the Himalayas, their bracing climate and the soothing green that envelope you leave nothing more to be desired. - Mahatma Gandhi

What was it about the Himalayas that held such fascination for me? Is that really such a difficult question to answer? I think that most people look at photos or movies that feature the Himalayas with awe and wonder.

But most people are satisfied to admire these majestic mountains from a distance, without the hunger for actually getting close and personal with them. Not me! I wanted to do something special - something relatively few people had ever done or would ever do. I wanted to walk in places that can only be accessed by foot. There are very few roads of any kind, good or bad, in the valleys in Nepal and even fewer that go into the mountains. So to get into the mountains rather than just viewing them from a distance, it is necessary to walk in on foot. That is exactly what I wanted to do.

In the ancient Indian language Sanskrit, the word Himalaya means abode of snow. And many of the Himalayan mountain peaks are covered in snow all year long.

Because of the continual snow cover on the peaks, it is difficult to believe that a huge shallow sea used to occupy the place where these mountains now sit. But it did. Of course, that was a long time ago – more than 30 million years ago. Yes, the Himalayas were formed between 30 and 50 million years ago. And yet, they are one of the youngest and tallest mountain ranges on earth.

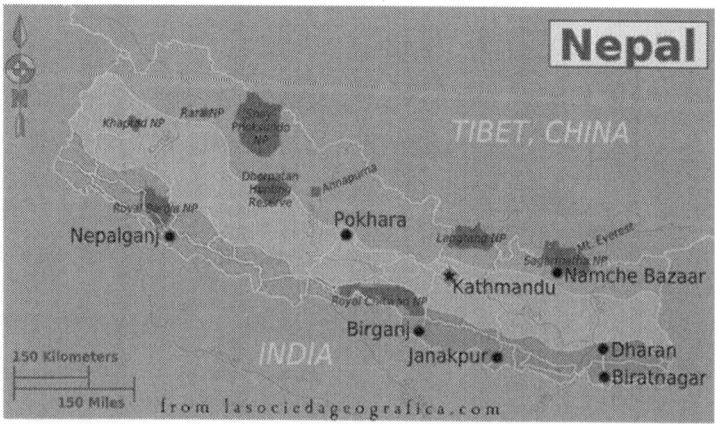

These magnificent mountains now form a border between the Indian subcontinent and the rest of Asia to the north. In fact, for hundreds of years, the Himalayas provided natural security to the subcontinent because armies could not make it across the high mountain passes in numbers big enough to be an invading force. Only very determined and very hardy traders and pilgrims were able to make it across the passes – and then only in a trickle.

The Himalayan mountain range consists of 3 mountain zones. The Great Himalayas are spread over the north of the range at the highest elevations and include snow-covered peaks that average more than 20,000 feet in elevation. This area is very inhospitable to people trying to eke out a living since very little can grow in such a cold climate with such a short growing season. There are small settlements in this zone, but the area is still very isolated and inaccessible.

The region just to the south is called the Middle Himalayas. Although there are some forests and fertile valleys, these valleys are separated by high, rugged mountains, making it too expensive to build good roads between towns. As a result, the area is only moderately populated, mainly in valley cities like Kathmandu, and also in some hill towns.

The range along the south is the Sub-Himalayas, consisting of foothills, plains, and long, flat-bottomed valleys. This area once consisted of forests that were inhabited by wild animals, including tigers, leopards, rhinoceroses, and deer.

But the habitat for these animals has been devastated because most of the forests in both the Middle Himalayas and the Sub-Himalayas have been wiped out so that the land could be reclaimed for agriculture. Because of this, the only area of the Himalayas that still has wildlife in any significant amount is the Great Himalayas – or protected sanctuaries in the Middle or Sub-Himalayas, such as *Chitwan*.

Colonel Jimmy Roberts, Father of Trekking in Nepal

When a person hears the word trekking, Nepal usually comes to mind because that is where trekking as an outdoor hiking activity for adventure travelers became famous. Trekkers in Nepal follow trails that have been used by Nepali villagers for centuries as the trading routes between Tibet and Nepal. These pathways were used long before anyone ever thought of trekking for pleasure or exercise.

So where did the word trek come from? It is an Afrikaans word which means 'pull.' By the mid-19th century, this word was already being used in English to mean a long arduous journey on foot and was later adopted as the best word for the adventure of hiking in the Himalayas.

It was 1949 when a British adventurer by the name of Bill Tilman got permission from the

Nepalese King to make several treks into some of the Himalayan mountain regions. Shortly after that, a French expedition trekked in the Annapurna region. But Nepal was not yet a household word.

It was when expeditions to the base of Mt. Everest began in the early 1950's that adventure trekking really started to become popular. And of course, when Edmund Hillary and Sherpa Tenzing Norgay reached the top of the world on Mt. Everest in 1953, Nepal was no longer known only to a handful of adventure travelers – it became world famous.

Colonel Jimmy Roberts, a former Gurkha officer and Military Attaché at the British Embassy in Kathmandu, had already spent years walking the hills of Nepal when he accompanied Tilman into the higher mountains in 1949.

Even though both Tilman and the French had trekked into some of the most beautiful locations in the Himalayas, they had not made any effort to develop trekking for the general public.

Colonel Jimmy Roberts

Roberts, on the other hand, recognized the possibility that trekking would attract tourists and would, therefore, be good for Nepal. As a result, he founded Mountain Travel in 1964, the first trekking company in Nepal and the inspiration for the adventure travel industry worldwide. Now, he is generally recognized as the father of trekking in Nepal.

His idea to provide tents for sleeping and Sherpas to guide and cook was revolutionary at that time, but was immediately successful and made the Himalayas available to people who wanted to enliven their travel with a little adventure, but did not want to do full scale mountain climbing.

The word Sherpa actually means people from the east and describes an ethnic group from the eastern mountains of Nepal. Sherpas are direct descendants of Tibetan wanderers who migrated across the Himalayas in the 16th century and brought their language, religion, and customs.

Because of their high altitude adaptation, Sherpas were the perfect people to accompany trekkers and mountain climbers on their expeditions into the mountains. Their ability as porters is legendary.

The Jimmy Roberts' model of trekking is called full trekking and is common today. Groups trek 5-6 hours each day with just their daypacks while Sherpas carry all the equipment and backpacks. The trekkers arrive at the destination where hot drinks and a good meal are waiting. And when it is time to sleep, each person goes to a comfortable tent and snuggles into a sleeping bag that Sherpas have already warmed up with hot water bottles. The following morning, each person is greeted by a Sherpa with hot tea and hot water for washing.

Not everyone who treks in the Himalayas follows this pleasant routine. Many trekkers do teahouse trekking just as Kay and I did. The term 'teahouse trekking' sounds pretty swanky and comfortable. But as you will find out later in this book, neither one of those words, swanky or comfortable, applies to the typical teahouse trekking experience in Nepal.

Boris Lissanevich, The Father Of Tourism In Nepal

One of the most iconic characters in the history of Kathmandu and Nepal is the former ballet dancer and White Russian adventurer Boris Lissanevich. While Colonel Jimmy Roberts is known as the father of trekking in Nepal, Boris is usually recognized as the father of tourism in Nepal.

In the early 1950's, Boris was running Calcutta's famous Club 300, which he had established and which was frequented by society's elite from maharajas to fighter pilots. King Tribhuban of Nepal was a frequent and popular guest. He and Boris became so friendly that when the King's son was going to be married, Boris was invited to the wedding. Of course, Boris accepted.

Boris Lissanevich

When Boris arrived in Nepal for the royal wedding, he immediately fell in love with the country and soon moved there. He opened the Royal Hotel in Kathmandu because he was sure that others would fall in love with Nepal as he had. He then persuaded the King that tourism would come to Nepal with just a little encouragement. And when the first wealthy tourists arrived there, Boris put them up at his new Royal Hotel. Later on, the Yak & Yeti Bar in his hotel became the central meeting place for climbers.

There were, however, obstacles that prevented many tourists from coming to Nepal. Visas were difficult to get and the time limit for stays was short. Boris decided to do something about this visa problem. After convincing a group of 20 tourists from Calcutta to choose Nepal as their holiday destination in 1955, he approached King Mahendra about granting 15-day visas instead of the usual much shorter ones.

After some persuasion, the King agreed, and those tourists from Calcutta who visited Nepal back in 1955 were the ones who inaugurated the real opening of tourism in Nepal.

And Boris stayed in his newly adopted home. For many years, he was a familiar sight on the streets of Kathmandu. His son Alexander has said that growing up with Boris was like leading a royal life. He recalled, "We lived in a large European style palace, with ayahs (servants) and lots of animals, from tigers to deer."

Unfortunately, Boris was unable to keep his businesses profitable. His main shortcoming was that he was too kind and generous. When visitors could not afford the price of a room at his hotel, he often invited them to stay as his personal guests. This, of course, was not the way to maintain a profitable business. Boris found that out soon enough and ended up losing his hotel.

Boris was a devoted advocate during his 30 years in Nepal. He died a legend at 80 in Kathmandu and was buried in the cemetery at the British Embassy in Kathmandu, Nepal, his adopted home.

The Nepali People & The Environment

Despite the harsh living conditions throughout much of the Himalayan area, nearly 40 million people live there. As might be expected, Hindus of Indian heritage predominate in the Sub-Himalayas to the south, and Tibetan Buddhists are predominant in the Great Himalayas to the north. In the middle, these two major groups have intermingled, and it is common to see signs of both cultures everywhere.

The eastern Himalayas are inhabited by people whose culture and animist religion is similar to people living in nearby Yunnan province of China and northern Myanmar. On the opposite western side of the Himalayas, people are generally Muslim with a culture similar to people of Iran and Afghanistan.

That is quite a mixture for a part of the world that makes basic existence very difficult. What brought these different ethnic groups to this harsh land? Some researchers say that famine or war in nearby areas forced people to move into the Himalayan area. Whatever the reason, the people have become hardy beyond imagination.

Most of the people have historically been dependent upon subsistence agriculture. Very few modern industries exist, and mineral resources are very limited. There is major hydroelectric potential in the Himalayas, but the combination of capital and skilled labor needed to develop it are not yet available in this difficult and daunting environment.

Literacy rates are low, malnutrition is common, there is a shortage of safe drinking water, and health services are scarce.

But improvements in transportation and communication, such as Western satellite television programs, are bringing Western influence, even to remote valleys where traditions and cultures had largely been maintained over the centuries, but are now being influenced in both positive and negative ways. For example, people are demanding and receiving better health care. But at the same time, they are losing pieces of their culture in an attempt to become more modern.

Tourism has played a role in bringing Western influence to many parts of the Himalayas. Trekking and tourism began to be important industries in the 1950's, and now close to 1 million visitors visit the Himalayas each year for trekking, wildlife viewing, and pilgrimages to Hindu and Buddhist sacred sites.

Since adventure trekking started in the mid-1950's, tourism has become important to local economy, but it has created problems as well. A case in point is the trash on the Everest trek. Many trekkers are environmentally conscious, but many are not. As a result, popular trekking areas have sometimes become polluted with refuse and sewage, and many pure Himalayan streams have become contaminated and undrinkable.

There are very few nations in the world that have such little road mileage and so few vehicles, so transport has always been by either porters or pack animals, depending on the region. In the Langtang region where Kay and I trekked, everything was carried in on the backs of porters, including cases of Coca Cola, Sprite, beer, bottled water, all cooking supplies, building materials – absolutely everything. No pack animals were used in this area when I was there in 1998.

Later, when Kay and I went on the *Ghorepani Circle* trek further west, I was surprised to see that mules and donkeys were used to carry those same things from the access road into the interior region. I was told that whether porters or pack animals were used to transport supplies depended upon the tradition of the area and the availability of animals.

The Caste System

Nepal, as a largely Hindu region, had a caste system and still does to some extent. But as was pointed out to me several times by Nepalis, castes exist all over the world – it is just that they are not official in most places. I encountered many Nepalis who were offended at being looked down on for having an official caste system when it was obvious to them that there were unofficial, social castes in most countries of the world.

The system in Nepal started during medieval times when it was brought into Nepal from India whereby Nepalis were divided into categories by an elaborate social system that dictated many facets of a person's identity, family life, food, dress, occupation, and culture. This caste system existed in most parts of Nepal for Hindus, but was not adopted by indigenous Nepalese or Buddhists.

One caste was considered intellectual and therefore able to rule. Another was considered strong and therefore given the role of the military. And of course, everyone has heard of the 'untouchables,' more correctly called *dalit*, who were the lowest of the low and could not enter temples, restaurants, shops, or other public places, could not go to school, and could not come near people of higher caste.

In 1962, it became illegal to discriminate against people of the *dalit* caste. Laws can change, but it take a long time to change people's attitudes, so discrimination still exists to one extent or another. For example, in the past, if a high caste person came in contact with a *dalit*, they used to bathe. Now they might sprinkle water on themselves as a ritual – or they might not care at all.

And because of changing economic conditions, people who were high caste now work in jobs that would have been beneath their status some years past; and lower caste people have been able to work in jobs that made it possible for them to become economically independent. Education is free and open to all castes, and all castes are supposed to be equally treated by the legal system.

So the caste system is still intact, but in a less rigid way. Discrimination today is mainly through social channels.

PART 2 THE TREK -
FULFILLING THE DREAM

Kate Benzin

Chapter 4 - Where Do We Start?

We live in a wonderful world that is full of beauty, charm and adventure. There is no end to the adventures we can have if only we seek them with our eyes open.
- Jawaharial Nehru

To Syabrubesi

Long before dawn, Kay and I made our way to Kathmandu's already crowded bus station to find the bus that would take us to *Syabrubesi*, the starting point for the Langtang trek.

Like many bus stations in Asia, people were frantically looking for the appropriate bus for their destination. And it wouldn't really be a typically Asian bus station without all kinds of merchants there to make sure that travelers did not start their journeys without the necessities in the form of snacks, candy, drinks, cigarettes, newspapers, magazines, and other assorted 'essential' items.

It did not take us too long to find the bus that would take us to Syabrubesi because our guide Furwa and our Sherpa Gurung had arrived long before us so that they could locate the right bus and take us directly to it once we arrived.

There were already lots of people on board, but we luckily found two empty seats together. It wasn't that we did not want to sit with locals or other trekkers, but we wanted to have time to chat with each other about our new adventure and what we were seeing outside the smeared bus windows as we rode along.

The bus was filled mostly with locals who were heading back to their home towns after visiting with relatives or friends in Kathmandu. Maybe some of them had even been in the big city to try to find work. In addition, there were a few other trekkers who were planning to tackle the same challenge that Kay and I were headed for - the Langtang trek.

So there we were bouncing up and down on springless, increasingly uncomfortable seats over rocky, unpaved roads for 10 hours on a local bus with Furwa and Gurung.

I looked around and saw that the other trekkers were so much younger. And they looked so fit. I wondered just how crazy I was. But of course, I did not voice my doubts about whether or not I could really do this - not even to my good friend Kay.

The bus ride itself was quite an experience. Nepal has very few roads, and the few that exist were not paved in those days. But the drivers did not seem to understand the logic of going slower when the road was rocky in order to preserve the integrity of the bus and the wholeness of the passengers. Instead, as private bus operators trying to make a living in a poor country, they would attempt to travel at speeds that would best be reached over the best paved super expressways. So the result over the unpaved, rocky, bumpy road was a ride that could easily put out your back. What an introduction to our trekking adventure!

But forgetting the temporary discomfort, the ride showed astonishing views, the most lasting of which was the terrain and its lack of any flat ground. I found it mind-boggling to imagine the non-stop, backbreaking work it took to survive in such an inhospitable environment, to terrace and cultivate the land, to transport products from place to place, most often on the backs of local people.

It was impossible not to think about how soft my life had been up to now compared to the effort needed just to survive there. Recognizing the amazing effort needed just for survival in that land of terraced mountainsides was only the beginning of a new perspective I was gaining on my own life.

As I sat on the bus and looked at the harsh environment, I thought about the way I had often complained about inconveniences that had seemed so major when they happened to me, but on reflection, proved to be as minor as they really were. For example, I remembered complaining so often about having to stand out in the snow waiting for a bus to take me to work. Instead, I could have just been thankful that I had a job to go to with a decent salary that paid my bills.

Or how often had I stood in front of the open door of my closet that was stuffed with the latest and greatest clothes styles and then complained that I just did not have a thing to wear?

When I returned, would I be able to remember how lucky I was to have a warm home and plenty of clothes to choose from? Or would I fall back into the same old routine and forget to appreciate what a good life I had compared to most people in the world?

These were the thoughts that I wrote in my journal when we stopped for breaks. And yes, I guess having been born into a middle class family in the U.S. gave me certain advantages that many people did not have. But at the same time, I recognized that I had made good choices along the way - it was not just a matter of luck that I was now in a position to have the freedom to travel to this exotic destination.

And tomorrow would be the start of the real adventure. Our guide Furwa told us that he would be waking us up at 6 or 7 a.m. to which we threatened serious bodily harm to him if he dared knock on our door before 8 a.m. I have always been an early riser, but I prefer to wake up naturally, without an alarm ringing or someone knocking at the door. This was, after all, a vacation

Luckily for Kay and me, Furwa was not a control freak who would try to push us to follow the routine that he followed with every other client. So he agreed to wait for us to appear at whatever time we wanted.

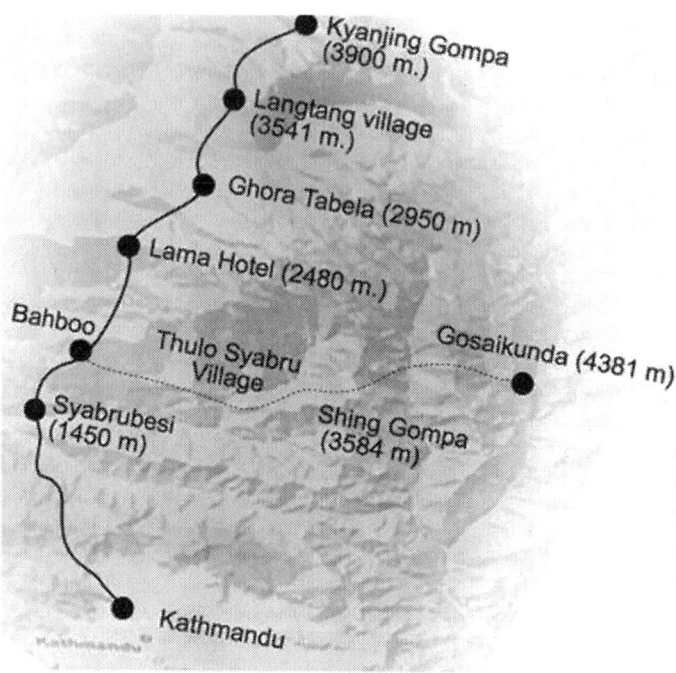

Langtang Trek Map

from blueyonderdesigns.com

Chapter 5 - Days Of Pain

When you travel, remember that a foreign country is not designed to make you comfortable. It is designed to make its own people comfortable. – Clifton Fadiman

Day One:

Syabrubesi to Bamboo, 8am-4:30pm, 4750 feet to 6500 feet

Experienced trekkers say that the third day is usually the worst. That is supposedly when your muscles rebel.

Well, how could the third day possibly be any worse than this first day when I could not believe how miserable I was? I was sure that there was no way it could possibly get worse.

But strangely enough, my problem was not the result of using muscles that had lain dormant for years. Instead, my problem was the result of lungs that had never needed to supply so much oxygen to my body in order to accomplish the task at hand.

As I already knew, I could barely walk and talk at the same time at sea level without getting breathless. Now on day one, trekking from 4700 feet to 6500 feet required my lungs to perform harder than they ever had before, and they were crying out in agony all day long.

At a particularly difficult point, Kay remarked 'Now you know why I never answer the phone when you call!' Of course, she was not feeling the pain that I was feeling, but she was trying to make me feel better – she saw the agony I was in and tried making a joke to take my mind off it.

In Syabrubesi, we had stayed at the Buddha Hotel, a no-star hotel which was the nicest accommodation that we were going to see until the end of our trip. Of course, we didn't know that at the time or we would have made a point to enjoy it more.

Our room at Buddha Hotel was very non-descript – a small plain room with 2 plain single wooden beds with thin mattresses. The communal bathroom was down the hall. But what made this hotel so luxurious in my eyes was the fact that the bathroom was actually in the same building that we were in. I did not realize that for the next several days, my middle-of-the-night bathroom excursions would involve getting out of my toasty sleeping bag, slipping my feet into cold shoes in order to head outside into the freezing air to find the separate bathroom building. What luxury to have a bathroom in the same building as our room – even though we had to share it with everyone else on the floor!

We started to leave Buddha Hotel at 8 am but were stopped by the owner of the hotel. And at this point, I would like to give profuse thanks to him. He stopped us to give both of us bamboo walking sticks.

He realized that we were complete novices and were totally unaware of what lay in store for us over the next several days. He knew that there were certain places where a walking stick might very well save a person's life.

Mine probably saved my life several times over the next 8 days. I soon found my new 'third leg' to be crucial in maintaining balance in places where one misstep could have sent me flying over a cliff to certain death.

This gentleman did not warn us of the dangers ahead or mention how foolish we were to head out without this valuable piece of equipment. Instead, he suggested in a warm and hospitable manner that it would be a very good idea for each of us to take a stick – and we could return them when we passed through at the end of our trek.

This was just one example of the kindness of Nepali people. And this man definitely chalked up some valuable points in the karmic scheme of things. So thanks very much again.

How is it that I missed the information about the importance of hiking sticks in the guidebook? Maybe it was assumed knowledge???

A bridge to cross -
thanks for the hiking sticks

I remember one particular spot that we encountered on Day Three where the path actually ended at a huge boulder that blocked the trail at the edge of a cliff. There was no way over the boulder. The only way to continue on the path was to scoot along the outer edge of this huge rock without looking down hundreds of feet to the whitewater rapids foaming at the bottom. This was difficult to do even for skinny people, but for me, it was monumental. And without my trusty bamboo walking stick, I would never have made it.

It was this particular event that motivated me to tell my close friends and family something very important the next time I saw them. I told them that if anything drastic (meaning death) ever happened to me while I was out on one of my escapades, they should realize that I would have died doing exactly what made me happy. How often do you get a chance to make that kind of realization?

According to the guidebooks, we were supposed to stop at Bamboo for lunch and then continue on to Lama Hotel for the night. Just who was deciding how far I had to trek on that day anyway? The days were mapped out in the guidebooks which all seemed to agree with each other and which trekkers viewed as the ultimate truth.

It was great to have the different treks outlined in the guidebooks, but did I really have to cover the same ground every day as a thin and fit 20-year-old?

I was planning to follow the guidelines like a good little girl, but ended up a failure already on the first day when it took me until 4:30 pm to get to the lunch stop, only halfway to the correct destination for that day. Horrors!

I couldn't have cared less whether I was at the right spot or not. All I cared about was stopping – and maybe even hoping for oblivion to relieve me of any further obligation to Kay, to Furwa, to Gurung, to whomever!!

So yes, I arrived at Bamboo at 4:30 pm – a bit late for lunch. Who could think of eating anyway? The altitude had already killed my appetite, and the gruelling effort to breathe was just about killing me. Enough for one day!

Besides, it was too late to continue on anyway. There was less than 1 more hour of sunlight. Getting to Bamboo had taken me twice as long as the average trekker.

I say 'me' because Kay, who had been living in Colorado at 6,000 feet and was much more adapted to the altitude, could have gone quite a bit faster. She could definitely have accomplished exactly what the guidebooks prescribed.

She was always way ahead of me. There was no need for us to stay close together. Holding her back to my speed would only have increased my feelings of guilt at not being able to trek faster. But we did want to end up at the same destination at the end of the trekking day. In other words, we wanted to be at the same place overnight – we wanted to share our experiences each evening.

So right from the first day of trekking, we fell into a routine where Kay would go ahead with our porter Gurung at her own pace. She was going much faster than I was, but as a competition – she was just trekking at a pace she felt comfortable with. Our guide Furwa stayed back with me and looked after me by trekking at my pace.

Each day in the late morning, Kay would get to our predetermined lunch spot and wait for me. She would walk around the area a bit to take photos or sit and relax or just sit and enjoy while waiting for me to catch up.

Once I arrived, we would each have a drink – Kay a Sprite and me a Coke. That turned out to be our lunch every day because that was all either of us wanted. The altitude had killed Kay's appetite as it had mine. It was about a 20-minute stop for me, but much longer for Kay since she had arrived earlier than me. But this particular 'buddy' system worked for us.

After having a drink, we would take off again, with Kay once again going at her own pace far ahead of me. She would then wait for me at our destination, and by the time I got there, she and Gurung would have arranged our room, and Kay would be sitting in the dining room chatting with other trekkers.

As guide, Furwa had the responsibility of arranging accommodations for us at the teachouses along the way. But since Gurung was far ahead with Kay and arrived at the teahouse before us, Gurung generally took care of that.

Luckily for me, Kay never felt that trekking in the Himalayas should be about how fast you could reach each day's destination. Instead, like me, she felt that the journey itself and what we gained from being challenged were the important parts of our adventure.

There were other trekkers who felt differently, people who seemed to feel that how fast they could do the trek was more important than what they were seeing and experiencing. I remember a man about 45 years old who was trekking with his two sons, both in their early 20's. All 3 of them were very fit, and they were definitely into speed – right for them, wrong for me – or so it seemed.

Altitude sickness, also called acute mountain sickness, does not care whether you are fit or not. In fact, experts find it difficult to understand why some people are susceptible to altitude sickness and others are not. But it is clear that changing elevation too quickly is an absolute no-no even if you are in excellent shape. And unfortunately for those men who had increased elevation too quickly, one of the sons got very ill and had to be taken down to lower elevation.

At high elevations, air has less oxygen than it does at sea level. Thus, it means that a person's body has to work hard to obtain enough oxygen to function properly. Altitude sickness can be the result when a person is not successful in getting enough oxygen from the air at high elevation, often because the person has increased elevation too quickly and not taken the necessary time to acclimatize.

Since I have already mentioned a little about my inability to walk on level ground at sea level and hold a conversation, I am sure that you can imagine the difficulty I had in breathing throughout this trek. There was never more than a step or two of level ground. It was always up and down, up and down. And I was continually out of breath.

At first, I was happy when I would come upon a downward stretch. Yes, I was happy – until I realized that going down only meant re-climbing what I had already climbed once, just to get back to the same level.

Kate Benzin

In her book Life Is A Trip: The Transformative Magic Of Travel, Judith Fein wrote –

Give me flat terrain and I can walk until the Messiah comes. But add a steep incline, and some exercise-activated asthma gnomes slow me to a crawl.

When I read those words, it rang so true to me. When I travel, I always do a lot of walking, but it is over relatively flat city terrain. My typical day when visiting a new city involves leaving the hotel around 9 a.m. and returning around 8 p.m. Most of those hours are spent walking around the city, getting acquainted with the new environment, stopping for a drink to watch people as they pass by, venturing down narrow lonely lanes, even getting lost and discovering special spots that I would never have seen if I had stuck to the advice in the guidebooks.

But now we were going up and down at high altitude, and it was arduous, to say the least. But I did not want anyone around me to realize just how difficult it was for me. I stopped every 4 or 5 steps. I pretended that I was stopping to take a drink of water, to unwrap a piece of hard candy to offset the dryness in my mouth, or to blow my nose. But actually I was just trying to catch my breath and give my lungs a break so they would not totally abandon me. I probably was not fooling anyone, but the pretense let me maintain a bit of pride. How could the local people actually live and thrive in this harsh environment?

The Langtang trek is not a loop like some other treks. Instead, you return over the same path that you took on the way up. In other words, a person can make the decision at any point to turn around and head back. It is not necessary to torture yourself all the way to the end.

And I'd had enough torture. I was going to convince Kay the next morning to turn back.

There was no way I could go on. At that point, I knew that the Himalayas had defeated me. I hated them. They were not going out of their way to persecute me – they were just standing there being their formidable selves.

Yes, I was the one who chose to visit these unyielding giants. They did not seek me out. Or did they? Hadn't they been calling to me for years? It did not matter – I was finished and I did not care whether my pride was wounded or not.

I did not mention this to Kay yet because I did not want to give her time to come up with convincing reasons why we should go on or to suggest staying another night to rest up before going on or to come up with some other alternative.

I was going back the next day and that was the end of that!

Day Two:

Bamboo to Lama Hotel, 9am-1pm, 6500 feet to 8135 feet

You can see from the sub-heading of this section that my determined plan to turn back did not occur.

Yes, last night my emotions and my body told me that I would not be able to face another day of trekking. And yes, I had secretly planned to convince Kay to abandon the trek and head back to Kathmandu.

Kay was very used to my suggestions for a complete, quick change of plans – it had happened before. And I had no doubt that I would be able to convince her this time as well.

But last night while I was lying in bed and still in the twilight zone of sleep, I remembered a previous day hike some years ago when I'd had the same feeling at the end of the day – that I would need a few days off my feet in order to recuperate. But then I felt unbelievable good the next day. I had been astonished that my body had recovered so well over just one night.

Even while I was thinking maybe the same thing would happen this time, I realized that I was several years younger at that time so I could not expect the same thing to happen again. And besides that, every bone, muscle, and nerve in my body agreed with me that I would never be able to do any kind of walking in the morning. In fact, I was sure that I would have to stay another night or two at the current teahouse just to recuperate enough to head back to Kathmandu.

So you can imagine how amazed I was when I woke up and felt no real aches or pains and no foot problems even though I had broken one of the most important rules of trekking, the one that says to make sure your boots are well broken in before starting out on trek. Yes, that is right. I had worn brand new boots. No chance to break them in because I had bought them just prior to our spontaneous departure.

So I did not tell Kay that I had been planning to return right away to Kathmandu. I kept it a secret just in case I would need to spring it on her later.

During breakfast, I wondered whether my feet were deceiving me and would only send signals of intense pain once I put my weight on them out on the trail. But no - my feet did not betray me. Not only that -- I did not have to stop to gasp for air as often as on the previous day. How was that possible? How could it be that just one day of trekking at this altitude would make an actual difference?

It still took me substantially longer than average to get to the destination that we should have arrived at on the previous day, but I did not care – life was good and I was in the process of fulfilling a dream that I'd had for years – a dream that had seemed impossible yesterday.

Besides, I arrived at Lama Hotel by early, instead of late, afternoon. In other words, I accomplished in 4 hours what the guidebooks said I should have accomplished the previous afternoon in about 1 hour and 50 minutes. Still slow, but major improvement.

At this point, you are probably wondering what the teahouses were like. To me, the word 'teahouse' had conjured up something in my mind that was not even close to reality. I guess I had not asked anyone for a real description of what the teahouses were actually like because I was a bit surprised at how just how very basic they turned out to be.

I was not expecting luxury, and I had certainly stayed in my share of dives over the years. But when I did, it was not usually freezing cold outside with no heat inside.

Well, not exactly no heat. There was always a source of heat and light in the dining room. Even with that source of heat, the room was not warm, and so everyone needed to stay bundled up in down jackets in order to be warm.

There's another phrase – 'dining room' – that conjures up something very different from reality. Picture a dining room. What is in your mind when you do that? Probably a lovely room with windows looking out onto a yard or garden – a table covered by a table cloth and some nice flowers – and so on.

Dining rooms in the teahouses did not resemble that picture at all. Instead, visualize tables made from various kinds of unfinished wood, benches made from the same unfinished wood, windows with the wind whistling through gaps in the frames, an old potbelly stove that was the only source of heat anywhere at the teahouse.

Teahouse dining room

The bathroom was in an entirely separate building. That meant midnight treks with flashlight for those of us who could not make it through the night without one or two bathroom visits.

No heat in any of the rooms – but what can you expect when you are paying only the equivalent of $1 a night – for a double room. So I was very grateful to an experienced trekker at the first teahouse who suggested that I get some water bottles filled with boiling water from the kitchen to put into my sleeping bag. I had bought a really good down bag in Kathmandu, so I put one hot water bottle at the bottom of my sleeping bag by my feet and the other one by my chest, and I stayed toasty all night long. Then the next day when that water had gotten cold, it was my drinking water. If you learn to listen, you can learn an awful lot!

The construction of all the teahouses that we stayed in was sub-par, sub-standard, and any other 'sub' that I could think of. The wind whistled through gaps in the window frames. Thank goodness for the hot water bottle trick. And thank my lucky stars that I had sprung for a great sleeping bag rated for Arctic weather.

I was also grateful to Kay who had brought along some little blue pills. No, not viagra, but over the counter sleeping pills – Unisom to be exact. My body was totally out of whack in many ways, one of which was an inability to sleep. That had never been a problem for me at any previous time in my life, but it was now – a common side effect of altitude. So Kay and I shared one pill every night, and then we both slept pretty well most nights.

Another way that my body was reacting was with a loss of appetite. Now this was a very welcome change. In the beginning, I thought that my appetite would probably find me again in a day or two, but it turned out that it did not return until we got back to Kathmandu. Here's what my eating habits were on each of the trekking days.

Breakfast – a bowl of noodles which I ate most of.

Lunch – Just a Coke. That was all I was interested in.

Supper – I always ordered something from the teahouse menu that sounded good. And the food at all the teahouses was actually quite good, but I would eat two or three bites and then could not force myself to eat more. The rest of the dinner went to our trusty guide Furwa and Sherpa Gurung who were very happy to get my leftovers.

They always got free food at the teahouse – their reward for bringing trekkers there. But they did not get as much as they wanted. So when I turned over most of my dinner to them, they were overjoyed.

We had a few snacks with us, most of which ended up going back to Kathmandu with us. The only snack I ate was 1 or 2 digestive biscuits at some point each day. Normally, I was a non-stop snacker – but not in the Himalayas. Maybe I should live there permanently.

My clothes were hanging off me by the time we got back to Kathmandu. What a great side effect of trekking! I went to a tailor and had some pants made. I still have those pants hanging in my closet in the hope that one day I will be able to get into them again. Only in my dreams, I'm sure.

The teahouse on this night had the same 'rustic' quality as the one on the previous night. Luckily, we were able to obtain 2 mattresses for each of our beds because one mattress by itself was pretty much the same as no mattress at all. Most of the mattresses at the teahouses were not much thicker than a blanket.

My side - typical teahouse room

By this time, I was seeing that personal hygiene just really was not as much of a necessity as I had previously thought. I think I adapted to this somewhat better than Kay. I could not be bothered changing my clothes. My cuticles were dry and cracking, and I found it impossible to keep my hands and fingernails clean. OK, I could live with that.

To be totally honest, by this time, I just did not care about cleanliness – and it was only Day Two. Was this just a passing phase? Would I regain my sense of caring about being fresh, fragrant, deodorized, and unsoiled after I acclimatized a bit? After all, I was still putting on full make up every morning. That showed that I had not completely lost my sense of standards.

But at least on this night, I was not scheming how to convince Kay to turn around. I was feeling pretty good about myself – even if I was not clean and even though it had taken me two days to cover the ground that should have been covered in just one day.

Day Three:

Lama Hotel to Ghora Tabela, 8:30am-12:15pm, 8135 feet to 9680 feet; Ghora Tabela to Langtang, 1:15 pm – 5:15 pm, 9680 feet to 11,600 feet

Up to this point, the terrain had consisted mostly of forest. I had been disappointed not to see spectacular views of the Himalayas, but I did not really think about it much since it took my complete attention just to put one foot in front of the other, and I had to keep looking down to be sure not to trip over any of the uneven terrain. If there had been any views of the Himlayas, I probably would not even have realized it at this point.

No, I had to keep looking down – a broken leg or sprained ankle would have been a major calamity as we were very far from medical help or even transportation. At this point, health care of any kind was several days walk away. What would happen if someone broke a leg or arm or worse?

The answer to that question became very clear a couple of times on this trek. At one point, I passed two men, one Western and the other Nepali, walking down very fast. Nothing too unusual about this except that they did not have backpacks, and they did not make the usual polite chit chat as we passed each other. In fact, they did not even make eye contact. So I just continued on the path.

Later in the day after we were sitting around at the teahouse chatting, a helicopter landed. The Western man got out, put his wife and young son on board, and took off. According to local sources, the boy had developed a severe case of acute mountain sickness, so the man had gone down to a place that had a 2-way radio in order to arrange for the helicopter. Also according to local sources, a person has to place a substantial deposit with authorities in advance in order to be able to get a rescue helicopter. Kay and I had not done that so we had no chance of being rescued by helicopter if the worst were to happen.

Later on Day Eight of our trek, we saw how local people are taken to find medical care. The person is put into a bamboo basket on the back of a porter and carried out to the road where we started our trek. That is where they can get a bus to the nearest hospital, which in those days was in Kathmandu. Remember the springless seats on the bouncing bus over unpaved road for ten hours. That ride was difficult enough on healthy people – what would it be like for someone in need of medical care?

That would have been the fate for Kay or me if one of us had gotten injured during the trek. Thanks again to the proprietor of Buddha Hotel in Syabrubesi for the life-saving bamboo hiking sticks.

Late in the morning near Ghora Tabela, I saw my first breathtaking mountain views. Now I remembered exactly why I had come to the Himalayas and why I was putting myself through the agony of trying to breathe in this high elevation, low oxygen environment. I came in order to see these exquisite, intimidating mountains up close. Every time I stopped and took in the view, I could not believe that I was really there – that I had really made it to a place that you can only access by walking several days.

And so now I had the perfect reason to stop every few steps to catch my breath. I no longer had to fabricate a reason. No one could challenge me for wanting to stare at the picture postcard view that was right in front of me now. I could have stood in one place all day just looking at those mountains. It seemed that I could just reach my hand out and touch them, but of course, they were still days and days away.

The setting at Ghora Tabela was so gorgeous that it was very tempting to stay there for the night, but this was the first day that I might actually manage to cover the distance that the guidebooks suggested for a day, and I wanted to prove to myself that I could actually do it. It was only 12:15 pm. Of course, it should have taken only a little over an hour to cover the distance to Ghora Tabela, so I was still way behind schedule. Just how realistic are those schedules in the guidebook?

Kate Benzin

But there were still many hours of sunlight left, maybe enough for me to get all the way to Langtang. So we continued on, knowing that there was still one more place called Thangshyap that had a guesthouse if Langtang seemed out of reach for me.

On we trekked. We arrived at Thangshyap, but unlike Ghora Tabela, it was not very tempting. The views were not spectacular like at Ghora Tabela, and the atmosphere was rather depressing. Still, I thought that perhaps we should stay there because I did not think I would make Langtang before dark.

But Furwa did not let Kay or me have a voice in making the decision. He became uncharacteristically authoritarian and said we had to go on – end of story. Up to that point, he had always negotiated everything with Kay and me – what time to get up in the morning, what time to start trekking, how far and how fast to trek.

So I was surprised at the change in his attitude, but later that evening, I found out that Furwa thought that some of the locals at that teahouse were of questionable character and that it was not safe for us to stay. That was why he insisted on continuing. Once again, I had learned the lesson of listening to local wisdom and not imposing my own judgment in new situations in foreign cultures.

At the time we left Thangshyap though, I did not know about the suspicious locals. I thought Furwa just wanted to stay on schedule. And maybe he was getting bored having to take care of such a novice trekker. No matter what the reason was, I walked away from Thangshyap with a sense of impending doom.

I realized that I my perceptions were a little off, and I knew that the altitude was affecting me, but I felt that my sense of doom was legitimate. I did not have a specific sense of what that doom entailed – it was just an overall sense that we were doing the wrong thing by continuing on. My main worry was that I did not think that I would be able to reach Langtang before darkness settled in and that I would be stranded somewhere without shelter.

The trails are treacherous in the daylight – I had to keep my eyes focused on the uneven ground as I took each step to avoid falling. How could I possibly manage once darkness fell? If a broken leg was in my future, I certainly did not want it to be here where there was no medical care and the only way out was on foot.

About an hour out from Thangshyap, I asked Furwa to go ahead and bring Kay back to where I was so that she and I could talk about the afternoon trek. Once she was there, I told her that I felt that agreeing to continue on to Langtang was probably the worst decision of my life. Those were my exact words.

Yes, clearly the altitude was playing with my head and my emotions, but I did not want anyone else to know that what was happening to me. I had made it this far, and I was afraid that Furwa would make us turn around and not continue the trek if he knew that I might be in the beginning stage of altitude sickness.

I could not really give Kay and Furwa a good explanation for my sense of doom so they convinced me that we should continue on. We then followed our normal trekking routine, with Kay and Gurung far ahead and Furwa staying back with me.

Since I was positive that I could not make it to Langtang before dark, I kept a lookout for a place where we could spend the night – a cave or a sheltered area of some sort. I was worried about spending the night outside even though Furwa was with me. I knew that he was experienced in camping out at altitude, but it had been snowing a lot and I was not looking forward to spending the night in the snow even with someone who could probably keep me safe.

Despite all my misgivings about continuing the trek from Thangshyap all the way to Langtang and my certainty that I would not get there before dark, the teahouse at Langtang came into view at 5:15 pm. Of course, all of my uncertainties vanished as if they had never existed, and I was as proud as if I had climbed all the way up Mt. Everest. I felt as though I had passed initiation – I had accomplished in one day exactly what the guidebooks said should be done in one day even though my day was quite a bit longer than the recommended time.

No matter that today's trek should have been only a half day. And it did not matter that I was totally exhausted, unable to concentrate, walking like a total drunk, unable to make the usual chit chat with other trekkers at the lodge, very disoriented. Yes, the altitude was definitely playing hardball with me now. But wow, I had finished a third day of trekking and arrived at the correct destination for that day.

Give the girl a gold star!

Kate Benzin

Chapter 6 - Time To Rest

If you reject the food, ignore the customs, fear the religion and avoid the people, you might better stay at home.
– James Michener

Day Four:

Rest Day in Langtang

Guidebooks advise staying a day in Langtang in order to acclimatize to the change in elevation. From Hotel Buddha in Syabrubesi to Langtang, the change in altitude is almost 7,000 feet, and the body needs time to readjust in order to be able to function properly at the new altitude.

In other words, no trekking today – finally the guidebooks gave some good advice that I could follow willingly unlike their timelines on how long it should take to get from point A to point B.

Many trekkers do not follow this advice. They are not worried about acclimatizing and so continue on without taking a rest day, but I was only too glad to comply. I could lay around all day long without guilt, without looking like a wimp – just following orders.

And as it turned out, the rest day came at a very fortuitous time. The night we arrived, I took my half of the little blue sleeping aid as usual, but it did not work, and I got very little sleep.

You see, a visitor came calling in the middle of the night. A small visitor, but a very noisy one. A mouse got into our cookies and dried fruit and made a lot of noise chewing through the wrapping and plastic. Not a big deal except that I kept waking up every time he rustled our goods.

When he did that, I made noises to scare him away. And off he would scamper. But then, every time I managed to get back to sleep, he came back gnawing at something in our packs, waking me up again. So I was on mouse patrol all night long, and so I was not a happy camper.

I think of myself as generally a pretty easygoing, rational person, but I am totally irrational when someone wakes me up in the middle of the night - even if it is for the very best of reasons. And this was not a good reason at all. I hated that mouse. How was it that Kay was able to sleep through all this commotion? She was usually a light sleeper, waking up at the slightest noise. And I was the one who could sleep through a bomb going off, but somehow not that night.

It was not until daylight that our nocturnal visitor abandoned his hunt, and mouse patrol ended for me. I was finally able to get some sleep.

Got out of bed at 9 am with swollen eyelids that were leaking fluid non-stop. Fluid build-up is a common side effect of altitude sickness. It is especially dangerous if it builds up in the brain or lungs. Luckily for me, the fluid coming out from between my eyelids was not life threatening.

In addition to this fluid leakage, my usual hypersensitivity to light had multiplied about a thousand times. I was disoriented, bummed out, freezing cold. What was I doing so far from vehicular transportation? How soon could I get back to Kathmandu? Thank my lucky stars that I did not have to go out trekking today!

And now, in addition to playing with my emotions, the altitude was affecting my physical abilities. I was shaky – I could not hold my hand steady enough to write. What a disappointment that was. I could not believe that the desire to trek in the Himalayas that I had been craving for so long might end so ungraciously.

I knew exactly what was happening to me, that both my emotions and physical body were not adjusting to the altitude. And I still tried to hide what was happening to me. Was I really fooling anyone? I do not know.

Then around noon, a miracle suddenly happened. My defeatist attitude disappeared suddenly and unexpectedly. My physical condition improved dramatically. I immediately saw all the beauty around me. Acclimatization kicking in. Way to go!

It was heaven to be able to hold the pen in my hand again and write words that were legible enough to be read at some future time. I could now enjoy the luxury of being in such a wonderful location – an experience that was even more meaningful for me as it was a place that very few Westerners would ever see. The exquisite view of the snow-capped mountains made all the agony of the past few days so very worth it.

I spent the afternoon relaxing, writing in my journal, chatting with Kay. And I did not think about what I would be facing the next day – the overwhelming challenge of trekking again.

But my mind did wander to some of the issues that Westerners are faced with when traveling in Nepal or other developing countries. For example, locals look at us and often assume that we are all wealthy. After all, we had enough money to travel across the ocean and come to their country. We have nice clothes and rugged shoes while they usually run around in ragged t-shirts, thin pants, and flip flops. In their eyes, we naturally must be rich.

There have been several occasions when I have overheard a Westerner say to a local merchant that he cannot buy a product because he does not have enough money. Maybe that is true, but it would be better to say that he just does not want the product because the seller will never believe that the Westerner does not have enough money for the item, whatever it might be.

For local villagers who may not have traveled to other countries, it is difficult to understand that someone who is wealthy in one country might not be wealthy in another. So Westerners just have to live with that misconception while they are traveling. For some, that is easier than for others. I myself found it very unpleasant, but knew that I could not correct that misunderstanding.

Locals also frequently believe that we all engage in the same activities that they see in movies, like carrying guns, having sex with multiple partners, and other dramatic behaviors used to portray Westerners in so many films.

Kate Benzin

I suppose it is inevitable that people from one culture will have inaccurate perceptions cross-culturally – in both directions. Like many travelers, I found it difficult to keep my mouth shut and accept that I could not correct those misconceptions during my short visit. Just one of the issues travelers have to deal with while they are on the road.

Chapter 7 - Keep On Truckin'

If you can find a path with no obstacles, it probably doesn't lead anywhere. - Frank A. Clark

Day Five:

Langtang to Kyanjin, 9:30am-2:15pm, 11,600 feet to 12,800 feet

Yes, I had acclimatized in Langtang, but the increasing altitude meant more serious problems for me. The terrain was actually easier to navigate than on previous days, but at this altitude, it just could never really be considered 'easy' for me.

In addition to increased breathing difficulties, my emotions were running wilder and wilder. The feelings of being defeated by the environment that I'd had the previous morning returned. I found myself trying to keep from crying all day long.

Once again, I recognized that altitude was having a negative effect on both my emotions and my physical condition, but I still did not want anyone to know the distress I was in as long as I could manage to hide it.

In trying to deal with what was happening to me, I kept feeling the urge to cry. I tried to hold back my tears, but trying to avoid crying in thin oxygen is not easy – or maybe it was just that the thin air made everything difficult.

Whatever the problem was, my efforts made a strange noise in my throat that alarmed Furwa, our guide. Thinking that I was having some kind of serious physical problem, he stopped me every once in a while to pound on my chest to make sure he did not end up with an unconscious client on his hands. I found out later that he was worried that my lungs were filling with fluid, and his pounding was an effort to push the fluids through.

Despite my plummeting emotions and my diminishing physical condition, I managed to arrive at Kyanjin in early afternoon. Once again, it had been worth every last breath that I struggled for. Kyanjin was an incredibly beautiful spot ringed by snow-covered mountain peaks. The setting was breathtaking. Even in my debilitated state, I appreciated the splendor that was all around me.

A German trekker commented that if this were Europe or America, this place would be totally spoiled with numerous fast food chains. He went on to emphasize how lucky we were to experience this pristine beauty. In discussions with the other trekkers, we all expressed the desire that this area would forever remain unspoiled by fast food restaurants and other modern amenities.

How very patronizing of us! That is so easy for us trekkers to say. We are here by choice. We will all finish our excursions and then return to the modern conveniences that we say we abhor, but choose not to live without.

It is true, though, that I consider myself lucky to have been in Kyanjin when it was 'unspoiled.' Part of the allure of travel for me is seeing exotic locations before they become 'modernized,' and I am sure that many other travelers feel the same.

At the same time, I think that it is important that we acknowledge that people living in 'unspoiled' locations have the right to bring in whatever modern amenities they would like to have without being chastised by Western travelers.

Kate Benzin

Chapter 8 - Going Down - What A Relief!

A Himalayan trek is a metaphor for life itself. - Yogavacara Rahula

Day Six:

Kyanjin to Langtang, 11am-2pm, 12,800 feet to 11,600 feet

Today was a big disappointment for me. This was the day of the final ascent. It was supposed to be the climax – a day excursion from Kyanjin at 12,800 feet up to the top of a 14,000-foot peak for even more glorious views and then back down to Kyanjin for a second night there.

Unfortunately, both my physical condition and my emotional state were deteriorating even more than yesterday. I'd had more breathing problems during the night. And in the morning, I had increased swelling around my eyes. The skin above each eye and below each eyebrow had filled up with fluid, and I had two little, fluid-filled skin-balloons hanging down over each eye.

I had been walking as though I were drunk on previous days, but now my stumbling had increased even more. Between the way my face looked and the way I walked, I could no longer try to hide the fact that altitude sickness was having a very bad effect on me.

Was this the doom that I had foreseen a few days before? Altitude sickness can have devastating effects on a person if he or she does not get down to lower elevation before permanent damage occurs from fluid filling the lungs or brain or else not enough oxygen to the brain. I did not have an urgent case of altitude sickness, but evidently every case has the potential to be very serious.

No one had to tell me that I could not trek up to the peak, but I knew that horses were available to take people up, and I was sure that I would be able to sit on a horse and hold onto the reins in order to go up and reach the summit. I was not being very rational, but I had come all this way, and I wanted to make it to the end.

Of course, once Furwa saw me, he immediately went into authoritarian mode again and rejected my idea about the horse and sent me back down to lower elevation at Langtang. He had enough experience with trekking newbies to know that he had to evaluate the situation quickly, take control, make the decision, and give orders – no discussion allowed.

How anti-climactic – to get so close without being able to finish. But I was in no condition to argue with Furwa. I could barely put 2 words together in such a way that they made some sense, so Gurung and I headed down to Langtang while Kay and Furwa headed up the peak. Furwa promised that he and Kay would be down from the peak in time to continue on downward and join us in Langtang in late afternoon.

I had started having altitude problems around 9,500 feet, but they were not too serious. It was going higher than 11,600 feet that had been my ultimate downfall. I had never been at that elevation before, so I'd had no idea that I would have such a bad reaction. I had read a little about altitude sickness, but I had always been the kind of person who thought that I could do anything once I set my mind to it – bad things only happened to other people. So even though I had read about altitude sickness, I did not expect to succumb to it myself.

Despite my dismay at not being able to finish the trek completely, it was such a joy to be heading down instead of up. Of course, it was never only downwards – it continued to be up and down, up and down. But at least now the overall trend was down, and that was a great relief.

Having arrived at the teahouse in early afternoon, I once again had plenty of time to ponder the emotions I was going through, as well as some of the issues that trekkers encounter on the trail.

One difficulty is that the long nights are often difficult to deal with. There is no electricity although sometimes there are camp lanterns in the dining area. Darkness falls in the early evening so there are a lot of hours of darkness to cope with if you want to enjoy the privacy of your room where you have only a flashlight for illumination and no heat.

If you prefer to stay in the dining room with other trekkers and enjoy having some light and heat and if you are feeling social, great. You certainly have allies who can relate to what you have been experiencing during your trek. But if you do not feel particularly social, then it is a matter of finding something else to do to pass the time.

Reading is one of my favorite pastimes and would normally be a great way for me to pass hours and hours, but because my mind was so jumbled, I found it impossible to concentrate enough to read. I was now at lower elevation and should have re-gained some of my sensibilities, but reading was still beyond my capability. In addition, I could not write much in my journal although I put in a few cryptic notes.

I no longer had those little balloons hanging in front of my eyes, but full recovery was still a day or two away. It was one of those times when I felt at odds with myself – not wanting to be off on my own, but not really feeling sociable either. I felt more comfortable being around other people even if I was not interacting with them, so I stayed in the dining room where there was a group of 10 British trekkers who I later found out traveled together once every year. I stayed by myself off to the side because I just did not have the energy necessary to get to know some strangers. Of course, I then immediately felt like an outsider because they were talking and joking with each other – obviously having a great time while I looked on wistfully from across the room.

I waited for Kay and Furwa all afternoon and into the evening, but they did not make it down to meet me. I was sure that if anything bad had happened to one of them, word would have reached me through the local grapevine which seems to be almost as fast as using a phone. So I was not worried, but I felt lonely and bored with so much time on my hands.

So without Kay and Furwa, I had time to think more about issues that I take for granted at home. For instance, I was not surprised that I was able to adjust to the lack of personal hygiene, but it surprised me to see so many middle class Westerners who did not seem to be bothered by their inability to stay as clean as they did at home.

I do not mean that we trekkers did not care about personal hygiene. But most of us put hygiene on a back burner for a couple of very good reasons. First, hot water was very scarce. And using icy cold water to wash hair or body was not appealing to any of us.

In fact, the freezing weather meant that even the simple act of changing clothes was something that none of us wanted to do. Most of us brought only one change of clothes for the nine days on the trek anyway because we did not want to add to the weight in our backpacks. And like the other trekkers, I saved my one set of clean clothes for my return to Kathmandu from Buddha Hotel in Syabrubesi where I could bathe. So on the eight-day trek, I wore the same clothes every day.

Day Seven:

Langtang to Ghora Tabela, 11:45am-2:10pm, 11,600 feet to 9,675 feet; Ghora Tabela to Lama Hotel, 2:30pm-5:30pm, 9,675 feet to 8,136 feet

I was still without Kay. I guess I was feeling better though because I did something that was not at all characteristic for me. I sat down next to one of the British guys by the furnace instead of plopping myself down at one of the empty areas. As soon as I sat down, he asked about Kay because he had heard from others that I had been waiting for her the day before. And it was just that easy – we started chatting away.

Another lesson for me. Why can't I remember that people generally respond positively to friendly overtures? I am always waiting for someone else to make the first move when I could just as easily be the one to initiate conversation. Over the years, so many people had told me that they originally thought I was a snob or just an unhappy person until they got to know me better – when all it would have taken would have been a friendly smile and hello instead of my usual looking the other way when passing by.

Still on my own this morning, I thought about all the different emotions I had been going through on the trek. In addition to the lesson of that very morning that if I would just reach out to people in a friendly way, the response would usually be positive, I found myself wondering over and over about why I was subjecting myself to the screaming lungs, to the dirt, to the sometimes boring nights, to the altitude problems, and more. What was I trying to prove? Was I trying to show the world how strong I was? Or how different I was from other people? Or perhaps just that I could actually finish something that I started?

That had always been one of my character flaws – starting a project, showing that I could do whatever it was and could even be good at it, and then going on to a new project before finishing up the previous one. That is how I have been with painting, playing piano, playing tennis, and so many other activities. And of course, on the first night of the trek, I was planning to convince Kay to turn around and go back to Kathmandu – after all, we had shown that we could do it. But for some reason, I did not give up this time, and I gave myself a lot of credit for that.

And then I remembered the exhilaration of being in Kyanjin the previous day with its gorgeous views, and I felt thrilled that I had been able to finish most of the trek. I was happy that I'd had enough presence of mind to take a couple of photos and to appreciate the spectacular setting even though I had been in the throes of altitude sickness. I recognized my good fortune for having been in a place that for a very long time will be seen by only the relatively few people willing to trek in – a place that will not easily be spoiled by the commercialism rampant in places that are more easily accessed.

In the midst of my musing, Kay and Furwa arrived late morning. The excursion up to the peak the previous day had taken longer than either of them had expected. And they did not get back down to the teahouse in Kyanjin until mid-afternoon – too late and too tired to continue on to meet me in Langtang.

Together again, we left Langtang to continue downward. The best thing about going down is that my lungs were not continually screaming for oxygen. The next best thing was that I saw what an amazing feat I accomplished going up to Kyanjin. Even though I was not able to do the last bit of the trek to 14,000 feet, I recognized with pride the feat that I had accomplished.

Even though I could recognize all that I had accomplished, there was a little gnawing at my stomach for not having done the final day hike up to 14,000 feet. And that little bit of embarrassment would not be eliminated for several years.

Day Eight:

Lama Hotel to Bamboo, 9am-11:30am, 8,136 feet to 6,500 feet; Bamboo to Doman, 12pm-2:30pm, 6,500 feet to 5512 feet; Doman to Syabrubesi, 3:00pm-4:30pm, 5512 feet to 4,750 feet

Today we made it all the way back to Buddha Hotel in Syabrubesi – not a luxury hotel objectively speaking, but after all I had been through, it sure seemed plenty luxurious to me. After all, we once again had a bathroom in the very same building as our sleeping room. I still had to put my feet into cold shoes to tramp down the hall, but at least I did not have to go out into the cold weather for my midnight bathroom visits.

On our way down to Syabrubesi, we passed through Doman and ate some of the best tasting oranges and pizza that I've ever had the pleasure to eat. I am not usually a big fan of oranges, but these were like manna from heaven to me. And it was amazing how delicious the local version of pizza was.

The pizza made me think about the effect that trekkers have on the local culture. Not only had foreigners taught residents to make a local version of pizza using whatever ingredients were available, but they had also exposed locals to many other things from Western culture. Whether that exposure is good or bad overall is not for me to decide, but traditions are being lost, local arts are not being taught to younger generations – the same process that happens all over the world when modernization takes place.

Over the years, I have had conversations about this issue with many travelers, who often speak disparagingly about the influx of Western things – fast food chains, clothes, movies, attitudes and so on. It is tempting to want places to remain unchanged and oblivious to the world around, but globalization is inevitable. It takes longer in remote locations, but it will happen.

In addition, there was always the dilemma about whether to hand out candy, pens, pencils, money for photos, and so on to adults or children.

The government of Nepal seemed to have already developed a bit of a dependent culture because of all the aid groups from other nations that had programs throughout the country – projects to educate people about gender roles, HIV/AIDS, general health, population control; projects to build hospitals, schools; projects to implement sustainable development.

Some of these projects are clearly laudable, but at the same time, some projects seem to be set up in order to instill Western values. For example, should we really be re-training locals about gender roles? As a woman, I firmly believe in the rights of women, but I question whether my Western view should be seen as the only correct one.

Kate Benzin

For years, hundreds of aid programs from countries all over the world have been set up in Nepal. I have always believed that help should be made to those in need. It is just difficult to know how much to help, where the line is that divides helping and imposing one's own attitudes instead of empowering people to make their own decisions.

Because trekkers are generally aware of the 'giving' that has been brought to Nepal by Western aid agencies, the topic of whether to give items to locals was often a topic of conversation among trekkers at teahouses along the way. Did giving pens just encourage more dependency? Did giving medicine indiscriminately to locals create the situation of covering up more serious medical issues and allowing stronger bacteria to develop? But how do you withhold medicine from someone who clearly needs it?

It was and still is a very complex issue, and I found it very difficult to withhold something that was so easy for me to give and meant so much to a local person.

So, many emotional issues to deal with in addition to the actual difficulty of the trek and the altitude. And I still do not have any answers to these questions, but felt that the questions themselves are worth considering.

Another thing I recognized was that even the hardiest trekker could not compare to the hardy locals who bathe and wash their hair in glacial water, wash their clothes by hand in the same frigid water, go about in skimpy clothing in freezing temperatures, and then turn around and put their hands into the blazing furnace to arrange the logs in the fire.

Day after day, I was filled with admiration for what local Nepalis have achieved over the years and what they continue to accomplish each day. My admiration started at the very beginning on the bus ride to Syabrubesi when I saw the terraces on the sides of mountains that were so steep that most people would have judged them to be impossible for any kind of agriculture. As a result of the steepness, some of the terraces were so small that those of us used to the expansiveness of the U.S. would have said it was not worth wasting the effort to cultivate them.

But different perspectives breed different results. Those steep mountainsides were all that the local people had to grow crops. So they put in terraces and cultivated them. The fortitude that it took to create those terraces in the first place and then to use them for farming year after year in such an inhospitable area made a lasting impression.

The next day, we boarded the bus to head proudly back to Kathmandu – once again on decrepit seats on a decrepit bus bouncing along over unpaved roads. But I had passed initiation – I was now an experienced trekker and very pleased with myself.

Kathmandu Again

The rest of our time in Nepal was certainly fun but uneventful compared to the trek. We spent time in Kathmandu, and like an experienced trekker, I advised people who had just arrived and were choosing a trek. The tables were now turned, and I loved being able to speak from experience about the challenges and beauty of the Langtang trek.

Our final celebration before heading home was a wonderful feast at Everest Steak House. The steak that I had at that restaurant still rates as the most delicious that I have ever tasted in my life. Was that because of the effort I had expended just prior to eating it? Probably.

You might be thinking to yourself that you thought Nepal was Hindu. And don't Hindus revere cattle rather than eating them? Yes, that is true. Many Nepalis are Hindu. Many Hindus are vegetarian, but not all. In addition, most of the Nepalis who are not Hindu are Buddhist, and it is common for Buddhists to be vegetarian as well. So what gives?

It turns out that having great steak restaurants in Nepal is another one of the side effects of tourism in Nepal. Modernization strikes again.

For Kay and me, a carnivore feast was the perfect way to finish our trek. We had earned it. And my appetite had certainly returned.

Kate Benzin

PART 3 - TRANSFORMATIVE EFFECTOF TRAVEL

Kate Benzin

Chapter 9 - The Real Accomplishment

By gamely crossing - and working to fortify - that bridge to people and to the places they inhabit, you weave more than a tapestry of memories and amusing journal stories. You tear down boundaries and form powerful emotional bonds; you come to know a place and its people. To me, that alone is reason enough to travel. - Lavinia Spalding, author, Writing Away

Over the years, I told many people about my experience on the Langtang trek.

I had consoled myself that not doing the last bit up to 14,000 feet was not all that important, that I had accomplished 95% of the trek and I should be happy that I had gotten that far. I was proud of what I had accomplished, but I cannot deny that every time I told someone that I'd had to turn back without doing that last little bit because of altitude problems, I felt a little bit of humiliation. I did not show it outwardly, but I am sure that my story lacked a little excitement in the telling because of that feeling of embarrassment.

It is like when many people compliment you about something – for instance, a new hair style. But despite all those compliments, if just one person says something negative about your hair, do you have in your mind all those compliments or do you re-run that negative comment through your mind over and over? Do you find yourself looking in the mirror to readjust a few strands to make up for that negative comment?

That was what I was doing about not finishing the Langtang trek completely. I kept re-playing thoughts in my mind that if only I had done this, that, or something else, maybe I would not have had the problem with altitude and could have made it all the way to the top of that peak.

Ten years later – although I did get somewhat fit and lose a little weight while trekking in Nepal, that did not last, and I quickly reverted to being out of shape again. And yes, walking and talking at sea level at the same time still made me breathless.

I continued to be a tour director, thus generating precious freedom for myself for months every year. Being able to choose what to do during my free time was wonderful. Sometimes I traveled. Sometimes I just worked on the business that I had started in Indonesia. The important issue was that it was my choice. Freedom from routine – life was good.

The Challenge - High Altitude Again?

Then, my employer asked me if I would like to open a new 13-day tour in Peru and Bolivia. That tour was in the Andes mountains, second in height only to the Himalayas.

I looked at the itinerary and saw that ten of the thirteen days would be at high altitude - several of them higher than the Langtang trek. Remember the little balloons of fluid hanging over my eyes, my stumbling, and so on? Logic would say that I should refuse this assignment which might end up with me getting altitude sickness once again.

Did I hesitate at all in accepting this assignment? Not even for a second - I said yes without a second thought. And I did not tell my boss anything at all about the problems that I'd had at altitude ten years earlier. If I had told her, she probably would have found someone else for the assignment. She could not take a chance that I would need to be replaced mid-tour because of altitude sickness.

There is no question that I was worried about being able to fulfill my duties on tour as leader of the group. It was not just that the tour was at high altitude, but that it involved strenuous activity at high altitude, such as difficult climbing on archaeological sites. It is true that there was no all day trekking, but as the tour director, I would not be able to take a rest day in order to acclimatize.

I became more concerned as the departure date for the first of two dry runs came near. A dry run for the top companies in the tour business means doing the full tour without paying guests in order to finalize all the little details and make any refinements needed so that it runs perfectly when paying guests are on the tour.

Before departing for Peru for that first dry run, I spent a week in Chicago visiting family and came down with bronchitis for the first time in my life. How did that happen? I had never had bronchitis before. It is commonly recognized that stress plays a big part in when or if a person gets sick. Was I stressing over whether I would be able to manage the high altitude? Maybe I got sick as a way to sabotage myself? Or was I just giving myself a good excuse in advance in case I could not handle the altitude?

It was too late to back out, so I made up my mind that I would just not let the elevation get the better of me again. Mind over matter – I was certain that I could do it. I think that somewhere deep inside, I wanted to eliminate that bit of humiliation at not making it up the final peak on the Langtang trek – perhaps this was my chance to get rid of that little bit of shame that had burrowed deep inside me.

This would be a new adventure – my first time in South America. I was going to see some of the wonderful places that I had seen in movies and photos. Machu Picchu, Cuzco, and Lake Titicaca were just three of the magical places that I would see on this tour – places that I had always dreamed about visiting.

At 8,000 feet, Machu Picchu was not too high for me, but Cuzco at 11,200 feet and Lake Titicaca at 12,500 feet would be real challenges for me. Would I be able to lead the tour? As the tour director, I could not stay in bed in order to get used to the altitude at my own speed.

Despite being very sick with bronchitis, I headed to Lima, Peru, to meet up with my colleagues to venture to high altitude once again. Throughout every last one of the thirteen days on that dry run, all I wanted was to stay in bed and sleep. I was so sick that I could hardly think straight, but I would not give in even though every step I took increased my pain and coughing.

Just like in the Himalayas, I did not want anyone to realize just how much I was suffering. I was worried that word would get back to my office, and my boss would realize that she had made a mistake in assigning me to this tour, so I covered as best as I could. I did, however, stay away from most of the physical activities that were part of the tour. When learning new tours, a tour director trains twice. And it is normal for the tour director learning the tour to leave all the activities until the second training.

That is what I did on this dry run. I assured my colleagues that I would do all those activities on the next dry run. By avoiding the strenuous challenges, I managed to keep it together to the end.

My colleagues were probably confused about my behavior - they may have thought that I would never be able to run the tour. But what was important was that I made it to the end. And I knew that since I had managed to make it through the whole tour at those altitudes, then I would definitely be able to do the tour and participate in all the strenuous activities next time through. My theory of mind over matter was winning.

By the time for the second dry run a few months later, I was back in good health. So that second time at high altitude in Peru and Bolivia would be the real test as to how well I could function as a tour director at that elevation. I needed to be a model for the members of the group, many of whom would be having their own problems with altitude.

Victory - I Did It!

Like in the Himalayas, I struggled with breathing, but so did most of the people in the group, and by stopping to chat with those moving slower, no one seemed to realize that I was in any distress. I participated in all the physical activities and no altitude sickness - even when higher than 12,000 feet.

So I continued with the plan that I would lead this tour. During the first few tours, I kept waiting and watching for the slightest sign that the altitude was affecting me. I guess that I was not yet 100% convinced that my mind over matter would work. But by the third or fourth tour, I no longer questioned whether I had won. I knew that I had succeeded, and that confidence stayed with me throughout the tour season.

Was it really mind over matter? I will probably never truly know what the secret of my victory was. I went on to lead the tour eight times during that year without even the slightest hint of altitude sickness.

I was many years older and even more out of shape, but victory was mine! And closure! Now I could tell my Langtang story, even the part that I did not complete, without any feelings of inadequacy.

Kate Benzin

Will I ever return to the Himalayas? I hope so.
Maybe one day I will write a book about how I
trekked the Himalayas at 80 or 85!!

Afterword

Often I feel I need to go to some distant region of the world to be reminded of who I really am. There is no mystery about why this should be so. Stripped of your ordinary surroundings, your friends, your daily routines, your refrigerator full of your food, your closet full of your clothes – with all this taken away, you are forced into direct experience.   Such direct experience inevitably makes you aware of who it is that is having the experience.   That's not always comfortable, but it is always invigorating. – Michael Crichton

The essence of this book dates back 13 years to the time when I was actually on the Langtang trek. I kept detailed notes about my feelings and thoughts each day. Most of what I wrote at that time has been used word for word in this book with further explanation to clarify what were sometimes very cryptic notes.

The Langtang trek was definitely transformative for me in ways that I may never fully understand. On the outside, I did not change much except for the loss of a few pounds, which gradually returned over the subsequent year.

But changes on the inside were more substantial and long lasting. What I managed to accomplish on that trek became one of the more important building blocks in determining who I am today.

Obviously, the story was not finished when I left Nepal in 1998. It was years later, when I was able to lead tours at high altitude, that I gained the closure I needed to understand the complete meaning of what I had done so many years before.

The spontaneous style of traveling that I enjoy works for me. If I had tried to plan out a trip to Nepal that included trekking in the Himalayas, I feel certain that I would have

Some people keep their journals about what they do - minute to minute, hour to hour, or day to day. I keep my journal about how I am feeling in relation to what I am experiencing or how I am reacting to those experiences. Yes, I wrote down events in chronological order, but the important notes that I wrote was about what was going on under my skin.

Thank goodness that I kept such detailed notes or else I might have questioned my memories. I might have thought that I was exaggerating my breathing difficulties or my reaction to the altitude. But luckily I have documentation from those days and know that what is in these pages is the truth of what I was feeling all those years ago.

Novelist and journalist Edward Streeter supposedly said something to the effect that travel is 90% anticipation and 10% recollection. I have found just the opposite. I think that those percentages should be reversed. I spend a lot more time thinking back on travel experiences, pondering my thoughts and reactions during the experience, and flipping through travel photos than I do on preparing myself for travel and anticipating what is going to happen. I might be unusual in that respect, but I would not have it any other way.

In the end, I fulfilled a lifelong dream. Not only did I accomplish more than I would have ever thought possible, but I can now look back and see how fulfilling this dream not only gave me a tremendous emotional satisfaction but also played an important role in the confidence that I needed at an important point in my life.

What motivates a person to finally take a stab at fulfilling a lifelong dream? How does a person know when the time is right even to attempt it?

When I look back on the time that Kay and I serendipitously ended up in Nepal, I had just changed careers for the umpteenth time - I had finally found work that would give me significant time off every year - I was feeling pretty happy with myself overall. Perhaps that is what gave

Kate Benzin

me the extra energy to attempt something that I had been dreaming about for so many years.

I am not sure that anyone can tell you when the perfect time is to do as Mark Twain advised, but I hope my story will resonate with you at some level to the point that perhaps you will feel motivated to take a closer look at your dream to see if there is some way that you can accomplish it now.

Nevermind if it seems that the time to fulfill your dream has passed – maybe that is just an excuse. I saw an 85-year-old woman doing the Langtang trek. She was not an athlete, but she was doing it. Her friends may have told her that she was crazy to go trekking at that age, but I can tell you that she was real inspiration.

I was recently reading a sales letter for a training program that was supposed to help me increase my business by quantum leaps. Here is part of that sales letter:

"You can live your life in the Himalayas or in the flatlands.

"If you choose to take inspired action, make bold moves and go for quantum leaps on a regular basis as an entrepreneur, you will surely find yourself experiencing what I call 'The Himalayas.' You'll experience breathtaking joys and amazing highs that will be the peaks you look back on near the end of your life . . .

"But of course they'll be some lows too.

"If you stay in the flatlands, playing it safe, taking small incremental steps toward your goals, overthinking things that you know in your gut are right for you, you won't have to worry about those lows. But, you'll never experience the life-altering highs either.

"Which will you choose?"

I could not have said it better myself. What a coincidence that this sales letter came just when I was working on this book.

Think about fulfilling your own dream. Give yourself a chance to follow it and stretch yourself – reach for the brass ring. If you are unable to grab it, you will never be sorry that you tried – the important thing is to put your trust in your own intuition, your own dreams, rather than someone else's expectations of you.

Kate Benzin

Author

Kate's first book **How To Find The Heart Of Bali** received great reviews. Here are just a few extracts from the reviews on Amazon.

Karen said "Reading this book is easy because it's like having a conversation with a local about the place she knows and loves . . . "

Asian Aficionado said ". . .Ms. Benzin's book has the travel juices running again. With the ease and confidence gained from this book, I'm looking forward to Bali's sunshine, seaside, serenity. . . "

Magic said "By reading this book I want to rush to visit Bali to increase my knowledge and have a great photo opportunity. . ."

Indonesia has been my home for most of the past 30 years since 1982 when I arrived for a 3-month contract to train people as word processors.

Although I love Chicago and have been back many times, Indonesia became my home because I fell in love with living my life as an adventure in Indonesia. So I stayed on and taught English for 14 years.

When I needed a new direction in my working life, I changed careers and became a tour director which allowed me to continue living in Indonesia while working all over the world.

Now I spend most of my time writing in my home/office just north of Yogyakarta in Central Java which I share with my three dogs.

If you have any questions or comments, please drop me a line at kate@katebenzin.com.

Connect with me online:

Twitter: http://twitter.com/kategypsy

Facebook: http://facebook.com/kategypsy

My blog: http://www.katebenzin.com

Also by Kate Benzin

How To Find The Heart Of Bali

(available now at amazon.com)

The Modern Nomad
(available August 2012)

October 2012 – Look for the next book in the Modern Nomad series which discusses how to work and still be a nomad.

Get the latest information at www.katebenzin.com.

Continue reading on the next pages – an excerpt from ***How To Find The Heart Of Bali***.

~~~~~~~~

Kate Benzin

An excerpt from:

How To Find The Heart Of Bali

by Kate Benzin

Introduction

"The world is a book and those who do not travel read only one page." - St. Augustine

Bali is considered by many to be one of the most spiritual and enchanting places in the world. It can be the perfect place to have your dream vacation.

Maybe even a destination wedding or honeymoon.

If you are reading this book, then you are probably already dreaming about a vacation to Bali. Maybe you're wondering just what you would find there.

Bali is one of Indonesia's more than 17,000 islands, 90 miles east to west and 50 miles north to south. It is situated between Java to the west and Lombok to the east.

Bali is in the tropics just south of the equator, but it is not your typical tropical destination. Yes, it has all the typical amenities of other tropical islands, but there are 3 things that make it far more special –

- a rich and unique culture that permeates just about every aspect of daily life from the little offerings that are put out 3 times a day to the religious festivals that seem to take place just about every day somewhere on the island

- scenery that is beyond belief, from rugged volcanic mountains to lush verdant rice fields to beaches that provide some of the best surfing in the world

- warm, gentle people who take it upon themselves to make sure that you have a wonderful experience on their island

Bali has become one of the leading holiday destinations in the world. In fact, Arthur Frommer, famous for his many best selling travel guides, listed Bali at #3 in his 10 favorite travel destinations for 2012. Here's what he says:

'#3 Bali, Indonesia: This destination usually conjures images of lazy days spent in the tropical South Pacific. But Frommer finds cultural goings-on's as fascinating as the terrain. "A Hindu outpost in a Muslim nation, it is inhabited by some of the most gracious people on Earth, who invite you to witness their religious processions, wedding ceremonies and joyous funerals."' - Mary Forgione, Los Angeles Times Daily Travel & Deal blogger, January 25, 2012

Before getting into the meat of the book, I want to make it clear that this book is meant as an introduction to Bali. It is not a guide book. There are many excellent guide books available, and you will surely want to buy at least one of them for more detailed information.

I'm not going to recommend which hotel to stay at, which restaurants to eat at, which sites to see.

Instead, my aim is to talk to you just like a friend would. Imagine that you have just told me that you're thinking of taking a trip to Bali. I've been there many times and just want to give you the gist of what's in store for you.

Just about everything in the book is from my own personal point of view. I want to share all that I have gained from my many experiences in Bali so that your dream vacation will be everything and even more than what you hoped for.

I am a Westerner who has been living in Indonesia for more than 30 years, and I feel that writing from a Western perspective but knowing the country so intimately, I have special insight into what it is like for a Westerner traveling in exotic Bali.

Please visit my personal website at www.katebenzin.com or my publishing website at www.gypsyduo.com. And please email me at kate@katebenzin.com with any questions or comments you might have.

Kate Benzin

Transformative Travel in Nepal

Kate Benzin

Made in the USA
Lexington, KY
02 April 2013